DAUGHTER

of the

KING

DAUGHTER

of the

KING

finally
free

FRAN SPEAKE

Palmetto Publishing Group
Charleston, SC

Daughter of the King: Finally Free
Copyright © 2017 by Fran Speake.

For information regarding special discounts for bulk purchases, please contact Palmetto Publishing Group at Info@PalmettoPublishingGroup.com.

ISBN-13: 978-1-64111-036-5
ISBN-10: 1-64111-036-8

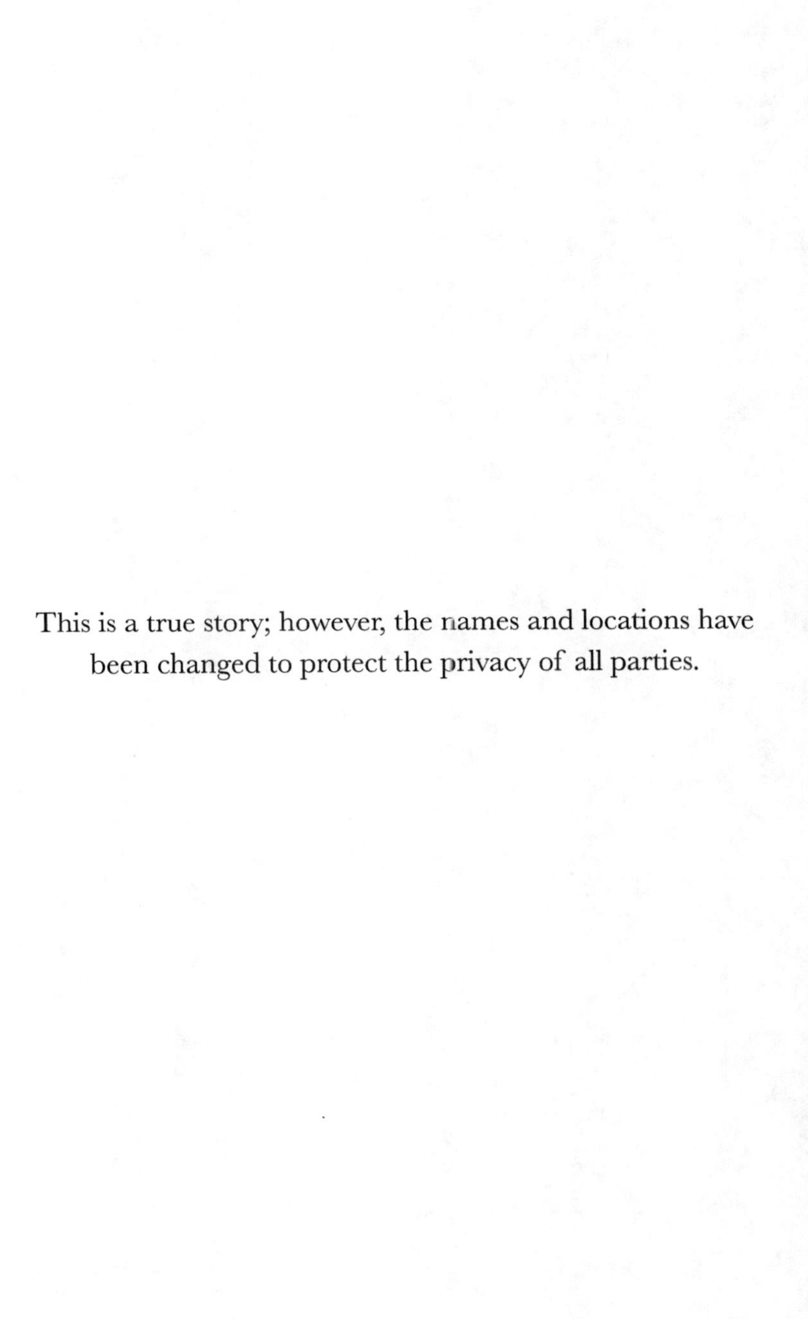

This is a true story; however, the names and locations have been changed to protect the privacy of all parties.

DEDICATIONS

To my Heavenly Father who created me for such a
time as this. Thank you Jesus for your unfailing love.

To my children, Jordan and Matthew...
the loves of my life and my greatest teachers.

To my mom whose strength I have drawn from my
whole life. It's not always been easy but I am glad we
got to grow together, I love you mom.

To my sister, Rody for your love,
support and constant encouragement.

To my sister, Rusty for caring for me so long ago
when we were so young, I will always remember
and always be grateful.

To my therapist, Bernie, who I laughed with,
cried with and healed with...you are my 'paeson'.

To my sponsor, Dona...thank you for your patience,
I love you very much.

To Carolyn, master at massage, spiritual guidance, health and
nutrition, I thank you for helping me to grow.

To Brenda, the best BFF any girl could have growing up.
Thank you for your love, loyalty, and honesty. I will treasure
you forever.

To Deshonda, there are no words that could do justice
for the love I have for you. Thank you girl for being a
true friend all these years and never giving up on me.
We will see that billboard yet...LOL.

To my friends Karen, Thara, Kate, Glynis, Delbis, Rob, Jeff,
RJ, Bobby, Vincent, Randi, Peggy and Sarah...you all have a
different meaning in my life and at one time or another you all
helped hold me together and I thank you.

To Rose, it was complicated but I will be forever
grateful that you have been a part of my life.

To my editor, Cassandra....thank you for the phone calls, the
encouragement, the feedback, the criticism...you know better
than anyone the blood, sweat and tears that went into this
project and I will be forever indebted to you.

And last but definitely not least, to all the people in recovery
whose path I have crossed, thank you for extending the hand
of help, I will surely pass it on.

In Memory
James Robert Speake
1938- 2010
I love you dad

I can do all things through Christ who strengthens me
Phil 4:13

"Experience is the thing of supreme value"

—Henry Ford

TABLE OF CONTENTS

FOREWORD

I first met Fran at a nursing home in late '97 or '98. She was the manager of a unit that was called the progressive care center or PCC. The unit specialized in caring for long term ventilator dependent patients who were deemed unable to wean in the acute care setting. I was new to Houston and was in the process of building my practice.

One of the things I noticed about Fran from the beginning was her loyal following of respiratory therapists that worked for her. Fran was very knowledgeable and so was her staff and thus, the patients were well cared for. The PCC had a family atmosphere and Fran would bring her children in to visit with the elderly patients who resided there. During the holidays they would go room to room singing Christmas carols. I witnessed a woman who cared and put her heart and soul in to her work, never looking on it as anything other than an honor to serve these patients and staff. This was and is rare in health care and what makes her outstanding.

Additionally, outcome studies done revealed the PCC achieved a seventy to eighty percent success rate at ventilator weaning, one of the highest in this type setting. Needless to say I was very impressed with her and the unit.

After medicare restructuring occurred, the decision to close the PCC was made, and Fran and a nursing administrator came up with a very aggressive business plan to open and operate a long term care nursing home specializing in ventilator dependent patients. There were none in Houston, however there was a strong need, and plenty of patients to fill the beds. I watched Fran gather information, write her senators and congressmen for help and advice, and put her energy and determination in to trying to make a difference and help others.

Throughout the years as we worked together and got to know one another, Fran opened up to me regarding her personal life. I got to know a woman who appeared to struggle from time to time with a form of perfectionism and she could be extremely hard on herself. I saw what made her a superior manager also gave her much grief. I am fortunate to know Fran and be able to witness her transformation that has occurred from walking in wellness. I believe no one deserves it more and no one has struggled more. I know Fran is a very determined woman, always trying to make a positive difference in someone's life but I now believe she will take care of herself too; her biggest obstacle has been defeated.

Abdul H. Khan,M.D.
Pulmonary and Internal Medicine Specialist
Cardiopulmonary and ICU Director
Atrium Medical Center

INTRODUCTION

But the Lord stood at my side and gave me strength, so that through me the message might be fully proclaimed

2 Timothy 4:17

WE ARE BORN, WE HOPE TO LIVE a good and pleasing life, and then we die. No one told me what would happen in between. No one told me what would happen when I die. No one told me how to live my life. Everything I learned, I learned by watching others. Because of this, I spent way too many years lost.

As I began this process the Conrad Murray murder trial was coming to a close, and I was reminded of the life of Michael Jackson. I can't help but compare the similarities beginning with the fact that Michael and I grew up in the same era, the 70's, with all the permissiveness that decade endured. We both had undesirable childhoods, alleged abuse overwhelming his and neglect in mine. Additionally, we both were treated for drug dependency after turning to them to fill an emptiness in us that, I now know, could never be filled by all the drugs in the world. I know, I tried.

Without giving too much away, I just want to begin with

saying that the basic love, attention and affection it takes to raise a confident child full of positive self esteem was nonexistent in my home growing up. When you do not experience love, you go looking for it, like the song says, in all the wrong places. From choosing all the wrong men, acting out with bad behavior, and consuming large quantities of drugs and alcohol, I searched and searched and always came up empty. I was, however, able to get into more peculiar and dangerous situations throughout these displays of tragic hunting.

Along the way, I developed a debilitating auto immune disorder, and have lived with it for fourteen years now. There is no doubt that I have lived and survived life. There is also no doubt that I have carried heavy burdens, guilt and remorse for way too long. Writing has enabled me to finally see the contrast of my life and let go of the unhealthy victim role I lived in.

My book begins with the horror I witnessed on my first day at a new job when I walked into someone else's nightmare. Little did I know at the time it was going to be another *thing* God used to get my attention, and get my attention it did. It became crystal clear after witnessing this horror, through prayer about the situation, that I was supposed to write a book to chronicle all the things I had survived, that the accumulation of tragedy that had occurred in my life would be beneficial to others. God was instructing me to do this, to be obedient. At the time I didn't know this, but obedience is turning out to be the key to all my blessings.

What I learned while writing this book is that the codependency in my life is what kept me in a very dark place, using drugs to cope with all that life was throwing at me, good and bad. I had the disease to please, a term I heard from Oprah. I learned that I became codependent as a child; due to the lack of nurturing and affection, I had no positive reinforcement to help me build confidence. I was constantly trying to be good enough, and to prove myself, always overly defensive of my actions. My self-worth and self-esteem was non existent.

It took me eighteen months after my Dad died, spending time alone, to really do a thorough self-evaluation, and to be patient and let God show me the things he wanted to do in and through me. I knew I was supposed to write a book, however I wasn't ready, and God had to prepare me. It took my dad dying for me to wake up to the realization that maybe I had been sober for a few years, but I was far from happy, joyous and free.

As with most things in life, we have to hit a bottom before we will make a change, and when I lost my dad, the impact was profound. The emptiness and despair were palpable and I was broken wide open. I became willing to do things a little differently and came up with my three R's, retreat, review and redirect. First, I took time off from the chaos, and retreated to a more peaceful place. I then reviewed my life, and while reviewing I asked the familiar question of why am I here and what am I supposed to be doing with my life? I am now redirecting, fully aware that the only one I can change is me.

Today, I do not suffer financial problems, my drug addiction has been arrested and I remain in recovery. My auto immune disorder is something that is managed now more accurately, not solely reliant on pharmaceuticals. My children are safe, healthy and happy. They love their mom and dad. My relationship with my own mother has never been better, something I could never have envisioned as a teen. Life is good.

My prayer is that by reading this book you will relate, and that my experience will help you in a way you would not have been if not for my story. I hope you will come away from this experience with hope about your own life. Hope that there is a greater force working for your good. Hope that if you are struggling with any of the things I talk about you will find your source of strength in God, not just find him, but get to know him and follow him, to trust that he will provide for you as he has for me, trust that he loves you as he loves me, and to stop struggling and let him have the reigns. You will never regret it. The moment you feel his presence or hear the whisper in your own ear, the peace is indescribable. So sit back, grab a hot co-coa and happy reading!

CHAPTER 1

For our struggle is not against flesh and blood, but against the
rulers, against the authorities, against the powers of this dark world
and against the spiritual forces of evil in the Heavenly realms

Ephesians 6:12

HIS BODY LAY IN THE BED contorted and motionless, the muscles contracted and forcing his knees into his chest, an unnatural pose in the fetal position. The plastic tube in his throat enabled him to breathe. His eyes were open but unable to follow any movements, saliva seeping out of the corner of his mouth. He wore a diaper because he was no longer able to manage his bodily functions. He lay there still, no longer identifiable as a young man, as if all the vibrancy of human life had been drained from his body.

Upon arriving to work that morning, I received my assignment for the day, my mind a little curious to see who this person with such a familiar last name was. I was a respiratory therapist in a smaller town in Texas where it isn't uncommon for me to see patients I know through a few degrees of separation. Normally my patients are a little older, but the name I saw jogged a memory. "Carte" is uncommon. People sometimes think it's "Carter" without the "r", like their ancestors just dropped it. I continued on my day, but it stayed in my mind.

After some research of my own, digging through the medical record and reviewing the patient I was about to treat, I discovered he lived in the same small county as I did. My mind kept racing, curiosity stirring so many questions all at once, "Could it be?", "No", "Maybe", "Oh my Lord, is it?" With all my years working in hospitals and critical care situations, nothing could have prepared me for what I saw in ICU 7 that day.

A middle aged woman sat in the room with him. She exhibited the sort of anxiety typical of hospital visitors when they're lost and don't know what's coming next. Her face was awash with familial worry. And yet, she put off a forced sort of optimism. As I calculated each step I was taking, I could see he was all of about twenty three years old. I looked at the woman and smiled. She looked like she needed it.

She smiled weakly back and that is when I decided I would ask.

"He doesn't happen to have a grandfather that's a judge in Wharton County, does he?"

She shook her head. "No," she said. "But his father is a judge there."

"Oh," I said. "I believe he resided over my divorce."

The woman tilted her head slightly, "That's my husband. I hope he was good to you."

Something came over me. I'm not sure what. As a people pleaser, I never say anything off color or offensive to anyone. But something made me say the words that so candidly came out of my mouth.

"As a matter of fact, no, he wasn't." I looked at the woman as all the pain of the past few years washed over me and I was struck numb. I couldn't fathom the odds that would bring this boy into my care. I couldn't imagine how probability and chance would allow this to happen. I stood there in shock and disbelief at how the man who callously took my children away would now be experiencing this horrific pain of his own, as I stared at his young son. And the odds-what were the odds that this boy would come into my care-particularly with this being my first day on the job. At that precise second, as I stood there stunned, I knew this was divine intervention.

The woman seemed to crumple from the inside. It appeared she could feel the things I went through over the past few years and all at once her head dropped, shoulders slumped and her eyes slowly closed. Immediately and without being aware of it, we forged a bond that neither one of us would have ever desired.

That woman and I began a two-hour conversation. I explained what my divorce trial was like. I told her how I had lost my children, that my husband violated court orders and even though I was supposed to keep it throughout the process, I lost my insurance. My ex spent our frozen retirement account on his new girlfriend. I was forced to have supervised visits with my children and this continued in spite of the voluntary drug testing I was submitting as proof there were no chemicals in my system. And I had given solid evidence that my children were being neglected, living in filth with their father, no attention being paid to their personal hygiene and being left alone, sometimes for days. And her husband did nothing. With all this proof, he did nothing. It seemed the more I offered up, the more he ignored it. I let my hurt and angst spill out. I allowed her access to all the feelings that had been boiling up inside of me because of how her husband unfairly dealt with my case.

And she, too, spoke to me. She vented about her son's condition. She told me the story of the accident, the Life Flight from Colorado, to Dallas, and eventually to my care. She told me that she never thought she would see her son like this. She told me she never imagined her son would die before her, but now she feared that the most. He was a newlywed and a youth pastor, and he had been hurt in a skiing accident.

In a strange way, I could identify with her. Though my children were still alive and healthy, they had been taken away from me in the divorce. We were two mothers commiserating together about the hand we had been dealt. We cried with one another as we recounted the pain we had each felt. In a peculiar way, we became like sisters, there in the room. We shared the pain we had experienced as well as hope for one another. It was emotionally raw.

I continued on my day, caring for the boy. As he lay there, staring at nothing in particular, a thought struck me several times. Over and over I kept hearing, *Vengeance is mine, saith the Lord.* I am not sure why I had that thought. I had no intention of hurting this boy. I am ever the consummate professional when it comes to taking care of my patients. Anyone who knows me knows I wouldn't harm anyone, much less a patient. It was my job to make this boy as comfortable as possible while he underwent therapy and that is exactly what I did.

I was struck with how that day turned out. How was I put into that situation? On any given day in the state of Texas, there are approximately 12,373 respiratory therapists. What are the odds this boy would end up in my care, especially considering he was injured in Colorado, then flown to Dallas, and then to Houston to the biggest medical center in the world, and then into my care? And all that on my first day at a new job. God was trying to get my attention. It was as if the pain had come full circle. The judge had taken away my children, and his son, as he knew him, had been taken away from him.

I walked around in shock as I finished my day. I couldn't believe what God was allowing me to witness and asking me to serve the man who had been so cruel to me. I could have changed assignments, but that never crossed my mind. I immediately sprung into action, knowing I would do everything in my power to give exceptional care to this boy who had absolutely nothing to do with my court case. It appeared to me that he was suffering from the sins of the father, and later, I would see controversial newspaper articles supporting this.

After taking care of this young man for about five weeks, I realized what I had to do. Through much prayer and meditation I heard God telling me to put everything together. It was as if He had laid out all these puzzle pieces throughout my life, and by meeting with the wife of the judge, he was telling me they needed to be put together. God told me to do something, and I knew I had to do it.

I had to go through the events in my life, and I was going to write a book about them to make sense of everything, to reveal the power and healing love of God. I wouldn't normally do that, as I'm not the type of person who wants to share deep secrets and dark pasts. I didn't want to open myself up for judgment from others, but I knew this would be for the greater good. I had to do this so that others could learn from my past mistakes and possibly save themselves from going through the things I had to go through. I knew that my lifelong search for love had wasted many years and if I could help someone find the answer quicker, it was my duty and privilege to do so.

I believe God saved me to write this book, to give testimony to his awesome love and power. He made me strong enough to endure all the hardships so that I could put this all down into words and give my story to others in similar circumstances. I lived a broken life, and was saved by God's grace and mercy. Taking care of that judge's son let me know that it was time to put it all together. It was as if everything I had been searching for my whole life had just been illuminated, and I was finally at a point in my life where I could see that.

I suppose, while I'm alive, I will never really understand all the reasons for the hardships in my life. I'll never comprehend why each one occurred the way they did. But I suppose that's the point. I'm not supposed to know. And the thing is, I don't care that He allowed me to encounter those obstacles. What I do care about is that I overcame them. I became the woman I am today because I didn't buckle. I became the woman I am today because I embraced the love of God, and filled my life with it. And I am grateful that I didn't have to journey alone, that He always has been and always will be with me.

CHAPTER 2

I know the plans I have for you, plans to prosper you and not to harm you, plans to give you hope and a future

Jeremiah 29:11

MY LIFE BEGAN ON NOVEMBER 21,1960 in Livingston, New Jersey. I was born to an Italian mother and Irish-mix father. We liked to call him a Heinz Fifty-seven. I had two older sisters, both with red hair, and then there I came, with a full head of dark hair. My mother finally felt she had an Italian looking baby. She suffered endless hours of labor and true to form, I was as stubborn back then as I am today, and didn't want to enter this cold cruel world. Aunt Gen, my great aunt, who happened to be a midwife, aided me in leaving the warmth, comfort and safety of the womb-a safety I spent years trying to recapture.

Now close your eyes and try to imagine the 1960's. Dwight D. Eisenhower was president, the population in the country was one hundred eighty million people and life expectancy was 69.7 years. Dow Jones high was 685, low 566; federal spending was 92 billion with the federal debt being 290 billion. Inflation was

1.4% with unemployment at 5.5%. The cost of a new home was sixteen thousand dollars, a first class stamp was four cents, a gallon of gas thirty-one cents, and a dozen eggs were fifty-seven cents. I was born at the tail end of the baby boomer years. The country's economy was thriving.

This was also the year of the first satellites; Echo One, communication, and Tiros, weather, and they were launched into space. Berry Gordy borrowed eight hundred dollars and started Motown Records. Harper Lee won a Pulitzer Prize for *To Kill a Mockingbird*. The most popular TV show was *Gunsmoke* and wouldn't you know it, the top movie of 1960, the year in which I was born, was *Psycho*.

Toward the end of 1960 people were hopeful about the future as a young handsome senator from Massachusetts obtained the democratic nomination for president. John F. Kennedy was elected president that year running against Richard M. Nixon. His son John Jr. was born four days after me, seventeen days after the election on November 25, 1960. Always the dreamer, I grew up imagining I would be his wife one day.

My parents moved us to Houston, Texas, the place where they had met, in 1964. They bought a home in Alief, a new suburb, in 1967. I had what I like to think of as an idyllic upbringing, although I now know that was far from the truth. I did the usual things a child would do. I played kickball with the neighbor kids, built forts, swam all summer long and had camp outs in our backyards.

My sisters and I, along with the neighbors' kids, even formed an all-girl singing and dancing act called the Sprights, combining our last two names, Speake and Wright. I was in love with Donny Osmond so all of our routines were to the Osmond songs, and naturally I took on the role of Donny himself.

My grandmother spent countless hours watching me perform Sweet and Innocent. Oh if they had only known, Sweet and Innocent was far from the truth, but fit well in my early years.

At no point in my childhood do I remember any violence in the house. Every day seemed calm and happy, however looking back, I have no real memories of sitting down to eat dinner with the family as we talked warmly with one another or everyday activities in the house. I do remember though seeing my mother with black eyes every now and again, but I don't remember asking about them.

The 1970's brought about my teen years and what I refer to as "Big D". My parents divorced when I was twelve years old. Up until that point I was a well-behaved, almost perfect child. After Big D, I became lost, angry, hurt, confused and unable to express my emotions. My parents must have been so caught up in their fighting that they weren't even aware of the responsibility of teaching us how to identify, much less express, emotions.

There was no caressing, back rubs or expressions of affection. Neither parent ever hugged us. The only adult to ever touch me was a male adult friend of my parents when I was around seven and this was extremely inappropriate.

Neither parent ever told me they loved me, or that I was pretty and could do great things. Something happens to a child when they are not shown any kind of tenderness or simple love, and in my case, I just shut down. At an already difficult time of entering puberty, this lack of affection and attention threw a monkey wrench into the whole growing up process.

My mother, God bless her, was so wrapped up in her own problems that her girls got neglected prior to Big D. I realize now she did so much better than what she was raised with. Putting a roof over our head, food on the table and clothes on our backs was Parenting 101, and in that class she earned an A+.

My father, who I loved so much was gone now. He was gone and I missed him. I was the only one who missed him and that separated me further from my sisters and mother. This is the place where I became the black sheep of the family since the others were extremely happy and I was completely distraught. Not once did anyone sit me down and explain the situation or ask me how I was doing. Not once. And you can forget anyone ever having the birds and bees talk with me. The limited amount I knew, I learned from the other kids in the neighborhood. I was aching, I was alone and there was no one to ease my pain so I suffered silently. Feeling void of emotion, I wasn't living; I was just existing and thus began my journey, looking and longing for love, accepting any attention I could find.

Marijuana and other illicit drugs were becoming very popular in the 70's. Until Big D, I was extremely against drugs, however Big D changed all that. The first time I tried pot was in 1973 when my sister Janice, with whom I shared a room growing up, and I, ran away for the first time. We had been grounded earlier in the week and knowing we weren't supposed to leave, we were restless and contemplated going out. I remember sitting in the front room right before my mom came home from work. We saw her car pull in the driveway. Our garage was in the back behind the house and Mom had to pull back there which left the front door accessible to run out without her seeing.

"It's now or never, we have to go," I said, my eyes darting back and forth from the back of the house to my sister, trying to follow my mom's movements and searching for an answer from Janice.

Reluctantly, my sister took off running and I quickly

followed, out the front door, down the street, over two more streets until we finally made it to the bayou, where we stopped to catch our breath. We made it to an apartment complex of a guy we went to school with, Carey, and he let us hang out with him. He was the one who turned us on and honestly, I do not remember feeling anything that first time but it opened up an explosive Pandora's box for me. Fear dissipated and the drug world was now at my disposal.

On this first adventure, my sister and I were only gone about eight hours, however this began a pattern of running away which led to being "kicked out" whenever my mother got angry at me. A tone was being set that neither of us were aware of and I felt disposable at a time when I really wasn't cognizant of any worth to my family in the first place.

Sadly, I couldn't figure out where I belonged in this world. There were so many moments when I found myself running away, either literally or figuratively and this is where my own fight or flight syndrome began. Over the years, I perfected both sides to this coin and being kicked out by my mother only seemed to fuel my insecurity and feelings of abandonment. I guess running away was all part of a greater search in my life. If I wasn't trying to get away, I was always looking for what was missing and if I couldn't find it at home, I was going to search elsewhere.

CHAPTER 3

*It is not the healthy that need a doctor, but the sick. I have not come
to call the righteous, but sinners*

Mark 2:17

ENTERING PUBERTY WITHOUT A MALE role model and being
the black sheep of an all girl family, left me longing for male attention. As with most young women in this same predicament,
I sought it out with all the wrong behaviors. I lost my virginity
right after Big D at the tender age of 13. As with the drugs,
once I violated that innocence, it became easier to do it over
again. And again. And again.

Nothing was sacred anymore, not that it ever was because
I had no concept of virginity and the pureness that came with
that. No one had talked to me about any of this. I had no
respect for my body. Once I realized that having sex would get
me "things", I knew I had an asset. I could now easily access all
the alcohol, drugs, and attention I wanted or thought I needed.

At one point my mother had started dating a very charming
Italian man. He was in love with the whole family, including
my elderly grandmother. I saw a side to my mom that was

foreign, and yet captivating. That hard tough exterior she had to assume as a young girl herself, was beginning to melt away. The tough bravado she had been forced to create was slowly dissolving like sugar crystals in iced tea, her callousness softening. I finally wanted to be at home when he was around. There was some peace in the house and I could actually feel the shift in mood. It was good.

I didn't know it at the time but the "good" feeling we were experiencing was peace and love flowing through our house, and to me it felt like nirvana. Instinctively, I knew I needed more. My mother seemed happy, and in effect, the rest of the house was too. Unfortunately, this man had some ties that were undesirable to being a positive Daddy figure in mid seventies family life in middle class America. I don't know to what extent, but he was linked somehow to organized crime and/or heavy gambling, always pulling out a huge wad of cash, the money being the sum of his worth. He and my mother soon parted ways.

I was devastated when they split up, but I then knew what it looked like to have a blissful mom in love. I found myself very attracted to all of this, that this man would take such an interest in our family, and actually wanted to be around and hear what was going on with us girls. Finally, some attention and healthy attention at that. Unfortunately, I would have to wait until my stepdad to see my Mom come full circle.

In the seventies it was safe, or so we thought, to hitch hike, talk to strangers and walk the streets late at night alone. My friends and I did this a lot. We snuck out of the house between the hours of 1am and 5am probably two to three nights a week.

On one of these junctures, I was walking from one friend's house to another's, where I was living during one of the times

I had been kicked out, and some guys stopped and asked me if I wanted a ride. Being tired and having *never met a stranger*, I accepted. I was young and naive, but a real red flag should have been raised when the passenger got out and asked me to get in the front seat between the two of them.

We started down Beechnut and hadn't gone more than maybe two blocks when the passenger pulled out a knife, thrust it against my throat, and anxiously began telling his friend, "Just pull over anywhere." Feeling the cold, serrated metal edge against my warm skin, my heart began pounding so hard I feared it would leap right out of my chest. Instantly I knew I was going to be raped and/or killed, and as I imagined my life-less body being tossed out, I couldn't help but think that no one would miss me, that I was dispensable. And being estranged from my mom, all I could think of was how disappointed she will be in me, again.

With my mind racing, I began to realize these guys must want what I was beginning to understand all men wanted, sex, and if I could give them that or make them think I would, I may live. My head was now spinning with the thought of my-self dead in one of the many open fields in Alief. There was so much undeveloped land that you had your choice of where to dispose of a body.

In a situation like this it is good to be street smart, and that was coming in handy now as I sprang into survivor mode, and my mind tossed around escape routes. I couldn't get out of the car, I was trapped in the middle of these two losers. So what does any young girl in a tragic situation do? Come up with a plan and offer to party with them. I knew my friend Lau-ren would probably be home because I had seen her earlier in the night. Lauren knew the streets better than me, but I was learning from her and she was quickly becoming my idol. And I knew if she was home, her dad may be there too. I knew if I could get there, I may live.

First, I told them they didn't have to do this, that if they wanted to hang out (code for get drunk and have sex), I had a girlfriend and we could go to her house and then there would be four of us. Now I didn't know if these guys were going to buy this or not, but I had to try something because I didn't want to be a statistic and lose my young life there, in such a foul, cruel and evil way. They went for it, hook, line and sinker. I really couldn't believe it, but I kept my composure and continued with the plan.

We headed over to Lauren's while the driver listened closely to my directions. The passenger had finally taken the knife away from my throat and I thought that was a good sign, that we were starting to build trust. We got in front of Lauren's house and I gave them precise instructions that I would go up to the door, knock and if she was there, I would wave them up to come in and if not, I would come back.

They let me out of their car and I walked calmly but briskly away from them, sensing their piercing gaze. Following my well laid plan, I nervously did exactly as I said I would except when Lauren opened the door, I hysterically mowed her over to get in and safe, all the while screaming, "Hurry close the door, these two men were trying to kill me, get your dad!"

Lauren's dad, Mr. Baldwin, was already walking into the front part of the house, and when I saw him, I frantically told him what happened, and asked if we should call the police before collapsing on their sofa. They both tried to calm me down with verbal assurances but the thing that worked the most was the realization of the gun in Mr Baldwin's robe pocket. In

1970's Texas, most everyone owned a gun and he was no different. He had picked it up at the first sound of tapping at his front door that night, realizing how late it was.

After about a minute and a half of trying to decide whether to call the police, one of the men came to the door and knocked. I held my breath as Lauren's dad answered the door; he had his hand on his gun, and it was safely hidden in his pocket and out of site, but still available should he need to use it to protect us.

I couldn't see which man it was but I heard the voice inquire, "Did a girl come in here?"

"Yes, she did," Lauren's dad answered.

"Is she coming back out?" the same voice then asked.

"No," Lauren's dad said flatly.

"Oh great!" the would-be rapist replied in a disgruntled tone.

That was it. No big scene, no gunfire or pandemonium, just oh great as he walked back to the evil infested car and companion waiting for him. Off into the dark night they escaped, my gratitude overflowing to Mr. Baldwin for saving my life.

How I managed to stay calm, come up with this idea and it work was beyond me.

My friends and I were traveling down a road to nowhere. We drank, did drugs, picked fights, skipped school and tried to intimidate all. I think the only ones who were not intimidated were the Harris County Sheriffs Department since we had a questionable reputation with them already. We hung out at our pool hall, Punk Palace, where we were known to win chugging contests against boys all the time. We definitely had the wrong kind of notoriety.

That same year, when I was fourteen, I found out from a mutual friend, Lisa, where some money was hidden in our neighbors house. She had money on her almost all the time, and not just a couple of dollars but usually a few twenties, which was unusual for someone in their early teens. One day I asked her where it came from. She told me about this stash of bills and exactly where I could find it, confiding to me how she knew about it. It was her friend who lived there and she had shared her secret with Lisa, telling her that it was her parents money that they kept hidden. She even showed Lisa where it was kept, but the problem was that the mom didn't work, and getting to it was going to be difficult.

How were we going to get her out of the house so we could get in? Leave it to my good friend Lauren to come up with what we considered the perfect plan. I had never done anything illegal other than some minor shoplifting but I was determined to get this cash. This was during a time I was not living at home, was attempting to pay my own way and never seemed to have enough money.

Lauren called the woman and pretended to be the school nurse and said her daughter was sick and she had to come pick her up. This gave us ten to fifteen minutes to get there, get in, get the money and get out. Luckily I had been given the exact layout from Lisa and could do this.

We decided another male friend would help me and he would be the one to open the window and hold it while I dove in. The problem we encountered was that we were almost out of gas and on the way over we had to stop and put in fifty cents, which was only enough for one gallon, and all the money we had between us. We had not anticipated this delay of stopping in the middle of this very serious crime, so now I was really scared about how much time we had or didn't have, but fear didn't keep me from breaking into these peoples house.

I did it with such precise planning and execution that you would have thought I was a career criminal. It was my first, and happy to say last, attempt at being a burglar, though. I was in and out within maybe 30 to 45 seconds and cannot describe the elation I felt when counting my "earnings" which totaled $1790.00. For a kid of 14, in the early 70's, 1975 to be exact, this was like winning the lotto.

I gave a lot of the cash away but I also bought myself a motorcycle, satisfying a love affair I had for years with street and dirt bikes. This dated back to when I was eleven and my sister saved up and bought us a Honda 50cc minibike.

The elated feeling of independence that money can bring was short lived because we had been identified. The mom had picked us out of a yearbook picture because two days prior to the real break in we had knocked on her door, and when she answered, we made some silly excuse of having the wrong house and left. However, we didn't know this yet.

It was January 1976 and I had moved home over the holidays. I was getting sick of this rogue lifestyle. Even back then I knew there had to be something better for me, and I was on this endless search to find it, directionless, with no one to encourage or help me.

I had gotten back in school and came home one day to find my mom and some people in the parlor. She called me in and said I had been identified in a break in where a lot of money was stolen. The mom had picked me out of a yearbook photo. It seemed, she recognized me and my male friend from our original attempt, when we knocked on the door. My mom, the cop and the other parents all spoke to each other but no one talked to me, they just let me know I was going to be charged. I was caught, and I was scared.

A couple of days went by and my mom said I was going to see a psychiatrist, to try and get some help. She had taken us to counseling once, right after Big "D", but all I remember is being with my two sisters and smashing these Styrofoam cups. I thought it was weird. I had no choice but to go, fully aware it would be a waste of my time, and my mom's money.

I found it strange when we pulled up to a hospital, not a medical building, but since I had never seen a psychiatrist before, I shrugged this off as not knowing. We walked into a big room, kind of like a waiting room and I remember seeing people sitting around and staring. We next walked down a long corridor and I remember thinking, *this is strange that his office is so far down this hall,* as I kept looking around for something familiar.

The lady showing us in opened a locked door with a key, and I still thought, *how odd* but it didn't register. Next, we rounded a corner and into a room, a hospital room with two beds in it. I looked up at my mom, my eyes searching hers for an answer, *what is this?*

My mom looked at me and began speaking softly, "There is something I haven't told you."

That was it. That was all I needed to hear when it hit me, all at once, like a tidal wave I didn't see coming, it knocked me over, and the shock and reality that I had just been locked up sunk in.

I felt my stomach knot up and my chest become heavy. The hurt I felt in that instant started to boil in the center of my being, and like fiery lava as it erupts, it began bubbling out and over every part of my body and very quickly turned to violent anger. I went crazy, and began yelling, screaming and cussing everyone out through uncontrolled sobs.

I cried myself to sleep that night in my new unfamiliar

surroundings feeling so completely alone, discarded and abandoned. I stayed there for two months, running away one time, but returning on my own after a few hours. It was the best thing my mom could have ever done for me and it was a sign that she cared, however at the time, I couldn't see it.

CHAPTER 4

We love because he first loved us

1st John 4:19

It was March 1976 when I was discharged from Bellaire General Hospital Psychiatric ward. While I was in the hospital, my mother sold our house in Alief and moved away. One of my sisters and I were still in school so mom found a way to keep us enrolled in AISD. Little did I know that the "Summer of '76" was going to change my life. I gave it that nickname and compared it to *Summer of '42*, the book, because I fell in love for the very first time and it would change my perspective on everything.

As I was discharged from the hospital, I felt a revived sense of hope-a clean slate of sorts and a chance to start anew. It was as if the old, dirty bath water had been flushed down the drain, fortunately not with the baby. The tub had been cleaned, and I was now soaking in a fresh bath filled with bubbles of happiness and joy.

My mom moved us to an affluent area, into a four bedroom apartment. It was an adjustment going from a house and neighborhood your whole life to an apartment. However, I seemed to thrive in this new environment as I was meeting all kinds of new characters. There seemed to be an endless amount of attention I could receive being the "new kid on the block" and I reveled in it.

The summers in Houston are so hot and the air is thick with humidity. People walk around soaking and each breath you breathe has the ability to scorch your lungs. Most of the activities during the summer included water sports, a way to beat the heat, and I chose laying out at the pool. While in the hospital, I was able to drop some baby weight and was starting to become a real woman with curves that even impressed me. With this new sense of self esteem and confidence, I bought my first bikini. I remember feeling really good about myself, my body and of course, the attention I was receiving from all the teenage boys in the complex.

I started hanging out and talking to a guy named Ted and quickly met his best friend, Brian. Brian was cute, really cute I thought, and he was so sweet. He was about five foot nine, thick dark hair, very muscular build and eyes you got lost in. He had definitely captured my attention, all of it.

I knew I wanted a better life than the one I had pre-hospital, but I had no clue how to go about getting it. I had no support or encouragement pushing me towards school, a hobby or anything constructive. No one in my life was actually paying any attention to me so the attention I got from Brian was the path of least resistance and the one most attractive to me. It felt like I could get the positive attention I had been craving from him.

Coming out of the hospital, my thoughts, views and beliefs had been transformed from the dark and negative to a lighter approach to life. My mind was like a dusty chalkboard, filled with scribbles before the hospital and now it had been wiped clean. I felt uncontaminated, like I was given a new beginning. I had lost that destructive edge while locked up and had no strong opinions now. I had this innate desire to do good and be good. I quickly saw that Brian wanted me to adopt his views and outlooks on life and for a time, it worked.

He played guitar and we would hang out, drink, smoke pot and sing. The thing that made Brian different was that he was very protective of me, something that I welcomed readily. Wherever we went, he was affectionate and never left my side. We were attached at the hip and wouldn't have had it any other way. The passion we felt for one another was red hot, like a firecracker, and our love was popping in all directions, radiating out to the world and each other. We would sneak out at night and into each others waiting arms, and eventually into each others bedrooms. He was saying the words I had so longed to hear....*I love you.* Someone loved me and I couldn't get enough.

Before Brian and this new ray of light came into my life, I had moments of contentment. I knew when needs were met and honestly, since Big D, I had experienced a few instances here and there of some laughter and a small bit of happiness when my mom dated the Italian man. More often than not though, I had lived with rejection, neglect and indifference in my short life.

With Brian, love came and knocked me upside the head and just like in the cartoons, I was dizzy and seeing stars. Creation came alive and while I floated through the field walking home after school, the flowers danced gently to greet me and the leaves politely bowed down to welcome me. The soft wind blew the birds' magical songs sweetly into my ear. Nature was capturing my attention and I was on top of the world. Where had I been for fifteen years? Why hadn't I heard or seen before now?

Brian and I could not get enough of each other, but I couldn't get enough of the drugs either. Brian turned me on to mushrooms because they were "natural". In his world, things that mattered were the Beatles, astral projecting (having an out of body experience), black lights, pot, and all the things that go along with being a hippy in the seventies. This was before all the "save the planet" promotions, but he was, for all intents and purposes, earthy. He was convinced the Beatles were the four angels, however I wasn't sure which four he meant.

After getting caught in my bed late one night by my Nana, Brian and I-driven by what we thought was everyone's need to control us-decided we had to be together for good, with no one telling us what to do or when we could see each other. It was 1977 and his parents were leaving for a job out of the country to work in Saudi Arabia. Brian and his brother, Bill, were getting an apartment so they could stay in Houston. We decided I would move in with him, however being only sixteen, I couldn't legally do this.

We approached my mom and dad (who were on good terms at this point post Big D) and made a very persuasive case. I informed them if they didn't agree, in a few months when I turned seventeen, I would do it legally and they would never see me again. Predicting a negative response from them, I was shocked but elated when they agreed.

At the time, it suited me to believe they wanted me out of their way and out of sight. I had definitely created friction at home in addition to the embarrassment I caused of being kicked out of AISD for cussing out the principal at my sister's graduation. I had taken my anger out on that principal, Mrs. Kelly, for sending my best friend, Isabelle away, and my family was justly horrified at my behavior.

For a while life was great. We were playing house and it was fun, but when I say I couldn't get enough love, I mean it. Enter insecurity and jealousy, two mean cousins.

These cousins quickly tore Brian and me apart. It was as if they were mistresses, however not his, mine. If Brian had a simple conversation with another female, I thought he wanted her and not me. Towards the end of our relationship, I came home one day to find Lauren lying on our couch with Brian sitting on the floor by her. I exploded and caused a horrific scene and with no basis or proof, I accused them of sleeping together. As unfounded as this was, it affected me physically and I felt like my heart was being ripped out of my chest while I also got sick to my stomach. This fueled in me another reason to feel abandoned as the cousins chipped away at my self-esteem.

Brian and I began to argue over the astral projecting and with a little liquid courage, I would get very confrontational, yelling, "If you can walk through the wall, do it now". I would create the most vile of scenes with my jealousy and insecurities, getting drunk and popping off at the mouth. There was usually no basis or merit for my explosions.

As beautiful as I was on the outside, I didn't feel it on the inside, and that was beginning to show. I had no self love and as a result, no confidence. I was losing a war waged by the cousins and it didn't feel good. The things that had drawn me to Brian, the differences, had now become fodder for my insecurity and jealousy. I wondered when things had gone so wrong? Where was all the hot burning love we had had for each other? That beautiful, endearing feeling I had for nature and the world, where had it gone? When did I become an angry person?

The hole in me was beginning to heal after my hospital stay and I was on the right track, but instead of staying the course, I got side tracked, thinking Brian would or could fill up the emptiness inside of me. This began a pattern I followed for most of my life that only now, can I even see or admit.

I do not believe Brian had changed, I had. Brian had continued to love me, and as he gave, I took. I had to have more and more as there was never enough love, attention or affection. I doubted myself and therefore I doubted his love for me. I demanded his loyalty and his faithfulness and he had to work day and night to try and make me believe. This was too much work for any human being. I really couldn't identify feelings or what was going on, I just knew when I saw him with another woman, I felt my heart being ripped out of my chest and stomped on and that I wasn't good enough or desirable. For a young woman coming of age, undesirable was the last thing you wanted to believe you were.

Needless to say, Brian asked me to move out about a year after we made that courageous decision to live together and spend the rest of our lives with each other. My heart was broken along with my spirit. It felt like the end of the world and I went into mourning. Here came abandonment again and it felt just as awful this time as it did the first.

CHAPTER 5

Blessed are those who hunger and thirst for righteousness, for they will be filled

Matthew 5:6

AFTER MOVING OUT OF BRIAN and Bill's apartment, I had nowhere to go so my oldest sister, Mary took me in for a few weeks while I sorted through my young distorted life. There I was all of seventeen, homeless, and a high school drop out with no direction.

While living with Brian, I had enrolled in the distributed education program at Robert E. Lee High School entering my junior year. I was going to school half a day, working half a day, and making my own life decisions. While I tried to keep up with this schedule, and did my best to act mature, I quickly became overwhelmed, and after a few short months, I quit school.

Right before the split I secured a full time position as a file clerk with an air conditioning and heating wholesale company in Houston. I was grateful for this little ray of light in my life since the break up with Brian saw my self-esteem taking another hit.

My sister Janice and I decided we would live together and rented a two bedroom, two bath apartment in southwest Houston. The party was on. During this time friends would come over and every weekend was a celebration, if only for the fact that the weekend had arrived. How I managed to be somewhat responsible is beyond me, but somehow the rent always got paid. I had a theory I lived by and that was pay the bills first and if there was only five dollars left over, then that was all you had to live on for the week. That was the extent of my maturity. Instinctively I knew that I had to keep a roof over my head, that no one was going to take care of me.

After moving out of Brians', I had reconnected with with a lot of the Alief crowd. The friends I had before the psych ward, Darryl, Lauren, Carol and Isabelle had remained close, and all but Isabelle had moved to Corpus Christi. Isabelle was still in school and I was very proud of her.

We didn't know it at the time but our friends had gotten involved in shooting heroin while living in Corpus. Isabelle and I used to drive down on the weekends and see them. We would all party but Isabelle and I did not share in the heroin habit. We were usually drinking, taking Quaaludes, smoking pot and doing any other pharmaceuticals we could get our hands on. Over the years I had developed an affinity for downers although I tried an array of agents ranging from black and yellow mollies; acid, including purple microdot, blotter and four way window pane; mushrooms; THC and crystal meth, better known as crank back then. Somehow, though, I always went back to the Mandrax, Valium, and Quaalude allotment.

Our friends in Corpus had met quite a few individuals they were beginning to consort with. One of these was a family of two brothers, Jay and Harry. Since I was newly single, I began a flirtation with Harry. What made it even better was that Harry had a never-ending supply of Valium, a drug I couldn't get enough of. Because we lived in different cities I never became Harry's girlfriend, but the attraction ensued.

On one of our trips down to Corpus, I remember Lauren having a bottle of cough syrup, Tussionex, the same thing as heroin, an opioid. I decided to drink some while the bottle was being passed around the car. Someone else told me how much to drink since I had never done it before. I drank and waited and this is where it all went black. I passed out and couldn't remember anything that occurred, woke up the next morning at some peculiar house, lost and confused. Where was Isabelle? Where was Lauren? Where was anyone?

As I tried to gather my thoughts and memory, Harry came into the room. I tried to be cool and not say much because I didn't know what had happened; I just felt something was amiss. The atmosphere had a sinister heaviness. Harry was acting strange and the innocent flirtation disappeared. Physically, I couldn't shake the feeling that something wasn't right but I was too embarrassed to say anything because, after all, I didn't know what had taken place. I felt an urgency to run. I needed to bolt from this nightmare I seemed to be waking up to. Thankfully it wasn't long until Lauren arrived with Isabelle in tow and we hightailed it out of there. I was silent the whole drive home.

Upon entering my apartment, I couldn't shake that gnawing feeling that I wasn't okay. Physically I was having pain. Emotionally, I felt remorse over not being able to remember what happened.

After discussing everything with my sister, I decided to call my doctor. He had me meet him at his office and he confirmed my worst fear, I had been raped and it had been anally. I sat there in shock and let the tears roll down my cheek. After a few seconds it became an outburst of horrific sobs each one stronger than the previous. Sobs for the little girl lost, sobs for the life that seemed to be slipping away, sobs for the feeling that no one cared or had ever cared about me and sobs for my purposeless journey.

What happened next was instinctual. Isabelle and I loaded up the car and drove to Corpus. I didn't wait for the weekend; we had to get there and exact our revenge. We arrived at Harry's house and I quietly stole a huge bottle of Valium. These drugs were his stash and his way of earning his filthy money.

We immediately left and came back to Houston. I was scared but too angry to let the fear keep my actions sound. Mentally I had entered a desperate realm and wanted justice and I was going to get it any way I had to. He was going to pay for what he did to me and no one was going to get in my way. By taking away his way of making a living, I was demanding the only kind of justice I had learned on the streets; get in, make him suffer and get out, quickly.

Most of the time I couldn't control my emotions or outbursts. I wasn't able to identify feelings as the only one I was up close and personal with, was anger. However I could remember a time before, when things seemed lighter, and not so troublesome. It was right after I got out of Bellaire General Hospital. I was starting on a road to healing and it had felt good. This turbulent journey was exhausting and now violence had to be tossed in. It had stopped being fun. I had to make a move in a positive direction towards the light and when our lease was up, I asked my mom if I could move home.

When most young people are getting ready to start out on

their own, I was doing the opposite and moving home at age eighteen, concluding my three year long experiment of being an adult. As I developed an assertive design for my life, which included moving home and signing up for college, my mom hesitated but ultimately consented to the arrangement.

I acquired my GED in 1979 and enrolled into the University of Houston Downtown, their version of junior college. This was a much needed boost to my self-esteem, to finally be moving in an honorable direction. Gearing up for college life, I decided I wanted to be a photographer and began to feel like I was worthy of a second chance, worthy of some hope for my future, and possibly worthy of some respect as I would be the only child at the time reaching for a higher education. It felt like I was getting off the crazy roller coaster that had been my life and was entering a more tranquil state. What a welcome relief.

At this time my mom and dad had been seeing each other for a year or so, post Big D. I guess like a lot of couples they wanted to see if time apart had changed each other or helped them to see things differently. I was in hog heaven as I had dreamed endlessly of having them back together.

I proudly enrolled in college, and my dad gave me my first 35mm camera, his old Yashica from his Army days. I secured a job at Wilson's, a department store where I worked in cameras and electronics. I was having the time of my life, meeting all kinds of new, responsible kids my age. I was learning how to create a dark room, what chemicals to use and like a sponge, I was soaking up this new found knowledge. I finally felt like I belonged somewhere. I belonged with my mom and dad furthering my education and trying to be the good kid that I was sure they wanted.

Unfortunately or fortunately, whichever way you choose to view it, my parents stopped seeing each other, but on the bright side my mom and I were finally getting along. It was only the two of us in the house and there was no fighting. We had acquired a mutual respect for each other. The years on my own helped give me an appreciation for my mom and her life struggles. Somehow I had acquired the ability to see from her perspective and from this view, I could envision what a challenge I had been. I believe my mom wanted me to succeed but she couldn't say it. She wasn't sure how to encourage as she had never been taught herself. We were entering new territory and although it was better, we still had a long way to go.

CHAPTER 6

Be strong and courageous. Do not be terrified; do not be discouraged,
for the Lord your God will be with you wherever you go

Joshua 1:9

COLLEGE LIFE AGREED WITH ME and I was feeling like a responsible teenager. Carol had moved back to Houston and we were hanging out whenever we could. She lived with her boyfriend, Kyle, in an apartment on the southwest side of the city and one night while I was visiting, some of his friends came over.

I caught the attention of one of Kyle's friends, Jamie. Carol called me the next day.

"Can I give Jamie your phone number?" she asked, adding "He really liked you."

"Which one was he?" I asked not remembering who was who.

"He was on the footstool where you were sitting and his cousins are Van Halen!" she blurted out excitedly, expecting me to be impressed.

"Who the heck is Van Halen," I replied rather sharply, not

realizing at the time they were an up and coming band who recently opened and toured with Black Sabbath.

After giving some thought to her request, acknowledging to myself that I was not dating anyone at the moment, I answered, "Yes you can."

Several weeks went by with no call and I continued filling my time with school and work. On one not so special day, Mom said that a guy named Jamie called, and that he had called several times, however he never left a message or number, only his name. So much time had elapsed that I had forgotten about him, so when Mom informed me of his call, I didn't know who she was talking about.

One afternoon when she and I were carrying in groceries, the telephone was ringing, Mom answered and said Jamie was on the phone for me. Frustrated by the evasive nature of his previous calls and weighted down by grocery bags, I picked up the receiver and sharply said "Who the hell is Jamie?"

I didn't realize it at the time but this set a conflicted tone for our entire relationship. My defensive nature was beginning to show and it wasn't very attractive.

Jamie and I had immediate chemistry and began spending all our free time together. Jamie was charismatic, funny and with him there was never a dull moment. He would pick me up in his van and we would go out to eat, to the movies and he would take me to and from school. We were inseparable. I would lie to my mom and say we had too much to drink, couldn't drive and this would allow me to spend the night with him.

I started missing school while Jamie became my new distraction and his attention was something I couldn't get enough of. I began to tune the rest of the world out and nothing seemed as critical as time together with our number one priority, catching a buzz. This was 1979 and cocaine was really popular; you could find it anywhere and we ingested our fair share.

We hung out with a lot of musician types at an assortment of clubs since Carol's brother was in a local band. There was an endless supply of alcohol and drugs along with unlimited drama, sexual adventures and intense fighting. Our entire relationship revolved around this gross display but I thought I had found paradise.

Not long after we started dating, his cousins' band, Van Halen, was coming to Houston to headline their first tour. I was excited but still not too sure of their music. I had grown up with The Osmond Brothers, Jackson 5 and the Beatles. I now listened to Lynyrd Skynyrd, ZZ Top, and Led Zeppelin. I even preferred females such as Linda Ronstadt.

Watching Edward, Alex, Michael and David that first year was electrifying and I witnessed what the world quickly saw, genius become superstar. Their music was unequaled at the time and Edward was quickly voted Best Guitarist in the World by one of the popular magazines. Riding in limos, attending the after parties and hanging out with them fueled my ever growing pride.

I recall one incident early on in which we had picked up Alex to go shopping, and a few blocks before we got to our destination, he and Jamie's sister decided to get out and walk. As we approached the store, Jamie and I got out as a crowd was gathering, everyone hungering to see what famous person was coming out of this limo. As we stepped out, I suddenly became aware of the mass of people and feeling extremely self conscious, I stared straight down, eyes fixated at the ground, and I ran in to the store. I felt the excitement in the air, at the same time sensing all eyes were on us, I panicked, not wanting to let the adoring public down with the fact that the real "star" was behind us by a few minutes.

There were many thrilling moments with Jamie's cousins, from sitting through sound check, partying backstage, attending the Texas Jam with other musician's, and the pride I felt for the whole family that their hard work and musical talent was paying off. Sitting with Jamie's family through the concerts, having funny family discussions over dinner and watching the band tune up are memories I will always hold close in my heart.

Jamie and I had an endless array of friends and hangers on. We were constantly at some level of intoxication, and within a few short months, to my shock, I became pregnant. Raised a Catholic, I understood abortion to be something they were against, however I had stopped going to church and Catechism shortly after big D. I had also not personalized any of the *Roe v Wade* controversy where abortion had been legalized so I had no real opinion for or against.

In the 70's we had endured the woman's lib movement and the burning of bras which had brought some men to their knees. I appreciated that women were acquiring a voice, and from my point of view there was no stronger female advocate than my own mother. Too scared at the time to inform her of my predicament, I gave her what she thought was a hypothetical and quickly learned she was pro choice. Identifying with my mother, my fate was sealed but first we dared to imagine a happy ending had Jamie and I kept the baby and raised her together.

I will never forget the drive to the clinic, the waiting room and then the table, the cold nasty table where they put me to sleep and executed this foul deed. While under, I had a horrible nightmare where these evil beings were carrying me, taking me against my will to some unknown place and I couldn't get away. No matter how hard I tried to wake up, or how loud I screamed, I couldn't escape the horror. I believe this recurring nightmare has helped me carry the shame of that fateful day for way too long.

Soon after, I moved out into an apartment in swinging singles Houston. I was so excited to finally have a place of my own and feel like a real grown up. I had dropped out of college and secured a full time job at the southwest home office of Prudential, one of the biggest insurance companies in Houston. My apartment was on the bus line so I could get to and from work since I had no car at the time.

Jamie would come over and spend almost every night with me. Living right in front of the pool, the party was on, and I met and made friends with all the neighbors. It wasn't too long after I moved that Jamie and I had one of our first fights. I cannot recall what it was about but I can remember the stitches I got in my forehead after he hit me and shoved me into a car in the parking lot, all after a long day of drinking. Of course we broke up, but we had just entered a realm of dysfunction that began a pattern of abuse I would have never envisioned for myself.

I moved from this apartment into a two bedroom with a girlfriend, Diana, to save money. Jamie was back in the picture because our "break up" lasted all of a week. We would stay up all night playing poker, drinking and hanging out with our friends. There was a revolving door with people coming and going. There were happy hours and not so happy hours with an endless amount of fighting between Jamie and me always concluding with visible bruises, scrapes and cuts.

Around this time, I lost my job at Prudential so I went and interviewed for a teller position at the National Bank of Commerce in Sharpstown Center, much closer to my apartment. They didn't want to hire me because I had no experience, however this is where I honed my persuasive powers and convinced the lady interviewing me to give me a shot.

With this moxie, I caught the attention of the bank president and he wanted to meet this very persistent girl, and with this, I sharpened my survival skills. To my delight, I became the darling of the bank and they were not sorry, my drawer balancing every day. Like most good things in my life, though, it was short lived.

I was beginning to realize that I would have to take care of myself, that no one was going to pay my rent, buy my food or even get me a car and so my self reliance shot into high gear. At this time, I had been taking the bus for about a year to and from, first Prudential, and now the bansk.

Working at the bank I met a lot of people and quickly made friends with most of them. Our head teller was looking for someone to take over her payments on her new 1978 Buick Regal. Once she knew I was interested, she informed me that she had about twenty seven payments left and they were $224.00 a month. I told her I had not established any credit yet, and to my surprise and delight, she had me sign an affidavit assuming responsibility. It read that if I missed even one payment, the car would go back to her.

I was euphoric, on top of the world and finally, I thought, a real grown up. Failure was not an option for me and every month come rain or shine, I found a way to come up with the money. I thought I had died and gone to Heaven in my new ride, equipped with bucket seats and t-tops. My joy was compounded when I received my first department store credit card with a hundred dollar limit. I was meeting all my needs or so I thought.

Around this time I went from one apartment to another, sometimes with a roommate, sometimes without. I would finish a six month lease and move on. At one point I had started a second job as a cocktail waitress at night so I could afford my car. Jamie lived at home to care for his mom and dad and at some point, he moved into his own apartment during one of our many brief separations. It was soon after this, during one reconciliation that I moved into his one bedroom unit. We couldn't get along, but we were so dependent on each other, we couldn't live apart either. Jamie and I continued to work, get loaded, and made fighting an art form. This was a time when we should have been on top of the world. We were young and in love and the world was at our feet. We were able to visit his famous family and we had even been invited to Edward's upcoming nuptials to Valerie Bertinelli, but instead we were miserable, the drugs and alcohol clouding our decisions and ruining our lives.

Due to our similar upbringing, and from a need to feel wanted, we had unknowingly forged a sort of bond. Jamie would change from being this wonderfully gentle man who was clipping and painting my toenails, giving me back rubs every day and night, to a monster with sudden violent rages that would leave me walking around with multi-colored bruises, cuts and scrapes scattered all over my body.

In addition, I was beginning to see that although Jamie worked as a machinist, he was an expert at drawing unemployment. Most of the time he would get mad, cuss someone out and quit or get fired, his short fuse uncontrollable. The stress on our relationship was almost unbearable. The criticism I would have to suffer from neighbors, co-workers and family members was taking its toll on me as I tried to hide in denial.

After one not so particular battle, as I laid there awake all night afterward, I asked myself, "What had happened?", "Why did we fight so much?" and most importantly, "Was this supposed to be my life?" The only question I could answer with any assurance was "No, this is not the way it is supposed to be."

I loved Jamie but I hated him when he got violent, and he was more violent than not these days. It was confusing and it hurt so much. He was two people, Dr Jekyll and Mr Hyde but I was too. I never let a fight go on when I wasn't violent back. He hit, I hit. He hit, I spit in his face (it's an Italian thing). I was a tomboy and a Texan, I was filled with anger and rage and boy did it show when we fought.

I clearly remember the only advice I got from my mom and she said "Don't hit back because that only makes it worse". By this statement, I subconsciously accepted my own dad's affinity for aggression and knew what my sisters had said was true, that my parents had fought and we had lived with violence in our home growing up. Even though I didn't remember the fights, it made sense. That is why I was okay with Jamie's violent side. I also knew as I lay there awake, I had to make a plan.

The next morning I acted normal as Jamie got up and went to work. The next thing I did was call my sisters crying out for help, and God Bless them, they both came running. My poor oldest sister, Mary was so upset that as she arrived, you could see her tears from my second story window as she got out of her car. Witnessing her reaction to my dilemma, it again validated what they told me and what I never wanted to believe about the violence in my own home. The door was barely cracked to that truth though; it would take many more years for it to fully open and for me to accept the entirety of the fighting that happened between my mom and dad.

We nervously packed up all we could and as one sister cried through it, the other was angry but there to help in any way possible. She wasn't angry at me for needing her, since my family knew from the bruises that Jamie had been violent; they had wanted me out a long time ago, so it was more frustration. Whatever had happened in the past I had refused to leave. Until now.

We were quick, precise, and were now moving out of fear. Fear of our dad, fear of the violence in our own house, and fear Jamie may come back and find us. This was combined with an overall sorrow of our own childhood cut short. These three grown women were now on a mission to save one of their own, one they loved and the youngest one who really had not the experience or memory the older ones had.

It is remarkable. We made it out before he got home, without incident, put my things in storage, and finally, exhaled.

CHAPTER 7

The Lord God said, "It is not good for the man to be alone, I will make a helper suitable for him."

Genesis 2:18

HOMELESS AGAIN AT AGE TWENTY, I attempted to evaluate my life however my state of mind was one of self pity. I thought I was done with Jamie and didn't know where to go or what to do. I had been living in a fog of alcohol and drugs. My sisters had their lives going well and my mom had met and was dating the man she would soon marry, my stepfather, Paul. I ended up staying with one friend or another and my world got much darker when I landed at the home of a girl from the air conditioning and heating company that I had worked at years before.

Deidre was a gay woman who shared a house with her lover, Susan and rented a room to her brother, Terry. Terry was ten years older than me and had just survived a divorce. I ate up the attention he gave me because my world was fueled by hopelessness, a feeling I was falling and that no one in my family was noticing the descent. I was escaping reality and living in a world so dark you could feel its diabolical nature everywhere with the intravenous drug abuse that was taking place daily. I was doing crystal meth and taking valiums to come down and Terry tended to my every need with his unending supply of benzodiazepams, my favorite.

Terry worked at a car dealership and quickly helped me get a job there. They hired me in the Accounting office and I was taught how to type up the new car make readies, in addition to relieving the PBX operator for lunch and her breaks.

Once employed, it was easier to regain that desire to do good and be good. It didn't take me long to move out of Terry's room and into an apartment of my own and as we continued to date, my drug use declined. All of a sudden I was learning how to really be a grown up and with Terry's help, I was working and not calling in sick. I could manage a checking account and pay bills as they were due, avoiding late fees. I actually planned and took a paid vacation, my first, to Hawaii with Terry, and we had a ball.

Terry had a positive impact on me but was not husband material because he had his family already, a beautiful boy and girl. Even if we had wanted to attempt a life together, he had undergone a vasectomy and I knew I wanted children. I had also suffered the ridicule of my mother while she thought Terry looked like my dad and accused me of having this sick father figure fixation. We stayed together for about two years and then broke up.

When I was with Terry, always in the back of my mind was this nagging feeling I was supposed to be with Jamie, and I missed him terribly. Jamie and I had gone almost two years apart from each other with barely a phone call. It had been good for me though as I had gotten a chance to see a different kind of life, one with a more normalcy to it, less fighting and no physical abuse.

My mother had married and celebrated her love with this huge wedding. My sisters and I gave her away. I was starting to believe I wasn't the black sheep anymore, trying so hard to fit in with my family...until the wedding.

At the reception there had been drinking but I had managed to pace myself and made it a point not to embarrass my mother on her day. There had been an exchange of words in the parking lot on the way out that night between some of my friends, but only words. Somehow this altercation had persuaded my mother to exclude me from the luncheon the next day that all my relatives were invited to. When I found out that everyone was told to keep it a secret from me, all progress at what I thought was fitting in, was lost to this gross rejection. My pain was palpable and I felt to be an embarrassment and disappointment to my mother, again.

It was hard to be alone in this world. I believe after the wedding, when I experienced the pain of rejection again, I changed. It was easier to go back with Jamie because he was saying he loved me and for someone who was aching to be loved, it was music to my ears. The time apart had faded my memories of the abuse.

Jamie and I began seeing each other again in late 1983 and by early 1984 we had moved back in together. We were now living in southwest Houston and Jamie was working for Joskes, cleaning carpets. I had not been able to hold a job longer than a few weeks since leaving the dealership. I had lost my beautiful car a few months earlier by simple automotive neglect.

New to our apartment complex, Jamie was making friends fast. Our drinking and drug use was escalating and so was our fighting. At one point we were living in poverty; even having our lights shut off. It appeared I was returning to the place that I had fought so hard to escape a few years prior.

One day in early spring, we had one of our knock down, drag out fights and Jamie left. One of the guys Jamie had befriended came by looking for him and I told him Jamie was gone. He asked me if I wanted to go with him to his friends and drink. Angry at Jamie and never missing an opportunity to get loaded, I happily accepted.

We were taking shots of tequila and he offered me a quaalude. I took it. I must have blacked out because the next thing I remember is coming to and he was on top of me, raping me. I looked around and thought "What happened? Where am I? How did I get here?" In my stupor, horrified at what this man was doing to me, anger boiling up inside of me, with both hands on his shoulders and with all my strength, I pushed him backwards and as he fell, I was able to get away. I grabbed my clothes, fumbling to put them on as I ran down some stairs, realizing I was in the same apartment, but he had carried me upstairs. I ran out the door and all the way home-home to an empty apartment, home to confusion, home to hurt, and home to an emptiness that was becoming all too familiar.

My mind raced. Guilt was beginning to consume me as I sat there contemplating what to do next. Nothing had stopped me, not intuition or a little red flag, nothing. I went with this man who I didn't even know. The next thing I did was go across the street to a pay phone and call my Nana. My grandmother was the only family member that had shown any amount of tenderness towards me so far in my young life and all I could think of was I needed someone to ease my pain and tell me what to do. She was livid when I told her what happened as I cried uncontrollably. The only thing she could do was comfort me by phone since she didn't drive anymore and I had no car.

I didn't immediately race off to the hospital or the police. I waited for Jamie to come home and I tried to tell him what happened. I guess after our fight I expected him to react with a soothing protection but he responded like he didn't believe me, slamming the nails into the coffin of that earlier guilt I had felt. Next, I called a male friend who was like my brother, and he came and took me to the hospital where I was examined and this outrageous violation documented. While laying on that cold hard table, I was reminded of the abortion and the coldness of it all had a sick parallel to my life and had me asking myself, where was anyone, why didn't anyone care about me.

In a desperate move to receive some kind of aid, to feel that I wasn't dispensable, I called my mother from the hospital and as I let the words "Mom, I was raped" roll off my tongue, she hung up on me. Horrified at her reaction coupled with the reality that the rejection was becoming all too familiar left me in a peculiar position in which I felt guilty for calling and waking her up. Her reaction though allowed the pangs of rejection and abandonment to seal their position in my life.

Later, I tried to take into account what a challenge I had been and make excuses for my family's desertion since my life seemed to be filled with drama. I would continue to believe that maybe I deserved this abandonment or that it was tough love, since there was no one to tell or show me different.

The next day the attacker came by our apartment, and knocked. Jamie answered the door and stated, "Fran says you raped her", posing it as somewhat of a question but also leaving it open ended. My reaction was violent and uncontrolled. I started screaming, yelling, and cussing them both out as I was so angry that Jamie didn't believe me and my own mother had hung up on me. I was so sick and tired of feeling rejected and abandoned. I was mad, madder than I had been in a long time--mad that it took someone who was only a friend to come and take care of me, take me to the hospital and show some care, concern and compassion. Needless to say, the rapist ran off as Jamie and I had another huge fight.

Afterwards, I called my sister, Janice and she came and took me to the police station to report the crime. They took pictures of the bruises that were all over my backside and upper thighs. They sent for the rape kit from the hospital.

Next it came time for me to be honest and through tears, I stated, "I went with him, I drank with him and I accepted a quaalude from him," believing I must have asked for this.

I will always remember and be grateful, until the day I die, for how the detective responded.

He said, "I don't care what you drank or what you took, this does not give anyone the right to violate your body without your consent." Finally someone who understood, who got it, who knew that I didn't ask for this. I could let go a little of that guilt I was feeling.

Unfortunately fear kept me from going through with pressing charges. The detective, my knight in shining armor, explained how the defense team would make me appear to be a whore, bringing up the abortion and pounding on the fact that I had left with this man, drank with him and accepted drugs from him. I have always regretted that decision and the lack of courage on my part to prosecute that vilest of creatures. Furthermore, the knowledge that a court appointed officer would try to make me look like the bad person in all of this has to be where my distrust for attorneys began.

After hitting the lowest of lows in my life, Jamie and I got away from that awful memory by moving to a new apartment that was open, sunny and airy as well as close to many businesses. With our new good luck at finding the place, I was able to land a job at another dealership that I could walk to. Life seemed to be turning around and we were coming out of the dark. I was able to buy a little used car from the place I worked at and we were on the upswing, financially, now that both of us were working. I started taking my Nana grocery shopping every Saturday. Afterwards, we would eat fried chicken and top it off with apple pie or ice cream before I would head home. Life was getting better...for awhile.

During late 1984 and early 1985, our newfound security seemed to help escalate my drinking, however, I found my drug use declining. With both of us working and the bills getting paid on time, it was easy to forget how bad it had gotten. The further we got away from the chaos of our former life, the more of a distant memory it became and I could justify drinking, after all it was legal.

I believe I was trying to be a grown up and prove I was responsible. If I could accomplish this, I may fit in with my family and prove I was worthy of their love. I had a natural desire for acceptance, longed for some familial normalcy and was still struggling with the need to be good and do good.

With all the demands I was placing on myself, I got really sick on Easter, 1985. I ended up in the hospital for a week with ulcerative colitis. I found out it was caused by stress. At the time, Jamie had been having what I believe was an emotional affair although I will never know if it was more. He started dressing up for his job and coming home late and I found out there was this girl at his work who was paying a lot of attention to him. She, like a lot of others, knew his cousins were famous and that always seemed to attract undesirables.

I believe the whole place knew about it too because I went up there one day and when I walked in, they warned him over the intercom system saying "Jamie, Fran is here". Trying to block his escape, I wasted no time in making my way up the stairs. I got to the top and saw the tail end of his shirt going down the back steps while I found this girl all alone, in the dark, one lamp illuminating her desk.

Shaking, I pictured him with her moments before, in the dark, sitting in the now empty chair in front of her desk, as they made the plans that lovers do who are having an illicit affair. Then a neurotic wreck, I chased him down the back stairs and as I caught up to him, he tried to brush it off saying, he just got in. Well we ended up having another huge fight and about a week later, Jamie paid me back by moving out on me while I was at work.

It was shocking to come home and find the place a wreck. All I could do was sit there and feel the pain of rejection, again. You would think with all the fighting and now possible cheating, this would be enough to make me run for the hills, but no. Within a few short weeks, I missed him and he was saying he missed me too.

We moved back in together and decided to get married. There was no get down on one knee and propose. There was no ring. There was no romance. The setting was opposite of what you imagine a marriage proposal to be. We were two very desperate individuals clinging to each other for some kind of normalcy, trying to do what was expected next, in the relationship. Unconsciously, we were putting on a facade, giving ourselves and the world what we thought was the natural succession of things.

There had also been a longing in my heart for a baby. I had been carrying much guilt and remorse over the abortion. I had this desire for a baby that wouldn't go away no matter how many times I tried to put it out of my mind. I guess I was still trying to fill up this hole inside of me and imagined a baby would help. It seems crazy with the wild lifestyle we lived, however in my world, you had to be married to have a baby and so the longing for a little one produced the wedding we hoped for.

Jamie and I went through the six months of premarital classes with the priest and I thought if the priest thinks it's okay, then it must be okay. With the exclusive help of my mother, we planned and pulled off a big beautiful Catholic wedding on February 15, 1986 at Notre Dame Catholic Church in Alief, where I had grown up. My mother agreed to give me the wedding of my dreams but it came with the unspoken agreement my stepdad would give me away. I greedily accepted this arrangement. I knew it was giving him a reason to live after his bypass surgery, but another part of me felt a betrayal towards my own dad. My selfishness won out though and I justified my decision with reminders of how my dad had not been there for me since Big D.

We had guests in from all over the country and as they attended a large reception in the ballroom of the Sheraton, I felt like a princess since all eyes were on me. How sad that the marriage was not as gratifying as the wedding. For a brief moment we had a reprieve from the chaotic lives we'd been leading with our beautiful day, but soon our old habits returned with a vengeance.

Jamie was having his friends over and at one point letting another couple live with us. He was getting more abusive and would go weeks at a time without speaking to me. Friends would come over during or after a fight, and Jamie would sarcastically say, "Look at the b**ch, just sitting there", adding "She's good for nothing." During these outbursts, I tried to maintain my composure and not cry from the humiliation.

I was abstaining from drinking or using drugs because I was trying to get pregnant but also, the lifestyle was getting old and it had stopped being fun. I was so unhappy and the final straw came after a fight, when I broke down in my closet. Holding a basket of clean laundry, I fell to the floor, crying uncontrollably, screaming out loud to anyone who might be listening, "I can't do this anymore!"

At that moment, I found enough strength to make a plan to leave. This time no sneaking, no hiding, I would tell Jamie I was sorry but I couldn't stay with him any longer. I wanted better for my life, more for my life, and somewhere, somehow I would find it. At that moment, miraculously I found an ounce of self love, just enough of what I needed to get out of this awful situation.

CHAPTER 8

For this reason a man will leave his father and mother and be
united to his wife, and they will become one flesh

Genesis 2:24

PLANNING AND MOVING INTO MY own apartment was the
most fun I had experienced in a long time. I had this triumphant feeling of independence. There was peace with no fighting, yelling or hitting, and no drugs or alcohol. I had gotten
the complex to put in new mauve carpet, and new appliances.
The atmosphere was bright, sunny and clean. I went out and
bought a new stereo, mini blinds for the windows and bedding
that rocked femininity, flowers and frills. My apartment was all
shades of pink and I was feeling alive.

The decision to get out and take care of myself had been
good for me. The courage I had demonstrated was a much
needed boost to my self-esteem and confidence. I was twenty-
six years old and envisioned that life had more to offer than
what I had experienced so far. More than anything, I wanted
to get mine on track and I set out to do precisely that. Thank
God for my stepdad, while he helped me obtain a divorce with

the *How to do your own Divorce in Texas* handbook.

I was working part time for my mom and collecting unemployment, having lost my job after two and a half years at the dealership. The day I was moving in to my new apartment, a tall, dark haired man had yelled out to me from across the parking lot, "Do you need any help?"

My mind filled with the pain of the last few years and with the anger I felt towards all men, I defiantly screamed back, "No, thank you!"

About a week later, I was beginning to mellow and relax, feeling liberated in my new apartment; I was laying out at the pool when this same tall dark stranger came out to meet me. He was slightly disheveled and I was struck at how he was dressed. It was August in Houston and as anyone who has ever been there knows, it is a sauna. He was wearing jeans, socks with tennis shoes and a tee shirt-no shorts, no flip flops, and no bathing suit. By the sweat pouring down his face, I could see he was miserable but also determined, when he courageously made that initial introduction.

His name was Johnny and he had just celebrated his thirtieth birthday. He was from upstate New York and sadly, he lost his mom three years earlier at the tender age of forty eight, to a sudden stroke. He came to Houston following a younger sister, to watch over her and had found work as an alarm installer. He seemed to be very outgoing and very interested in me. Only later did I find out he had been spying on me through a pair of binoculars from a neighbor's upstairs apartment. He seemed nice enough on that first meeting; however he disappeared for several weeks.

I was busy knocking on doors, introducing myself, determined to make new friends and leave behind the old lifestyle and relationships that weren't working for me. I was succeeding. I had met a girl across the walkway named Lori. She lived there with her boyfriend and she quickly became my new best friend when she introduced me to the neighbors that hung out together.

A few weeks later I asked her what happened to Johnny. He had seemed so interested in me that first day but maybe I read him wrong. Lori told me he was in school and she believed that is why we didn't see him. Later Lori ran in to Johnny at a party and casually mentioned that I had asked about him. Next thing I knew Johnny was coming home earlier and earlier, knocking on my door, and we would stand in the parking lot and talk for hours. During each of these sessions we were becoming close; emotionally as we learned more about each other, and physically as we sat on our cars, each encounter inching nearer to each other, eventually his arm crisscrossed behind mine but not touching. Ever the gentleman, he was making an impression.

One evening we made our way into his apartment and as we talked, I found out Johnny had recently gone back to school and was studying law. He had obtained his bachelor in psychology and masters degree in counseling from the State University of New York at Oswego. I started to contemplate the idea that maybe this guy would be good for me. He seemed extremely interested, he was educated and seeking more education, and I found out he had never done drugs. I thought to myself, *I have never been with someone like him.* I was intrigued while I dared to imagine a better life. I wanted off this roller coaster, and Johnny appeared to be a refreshing escape.

As we began dating, Johnny would invite me to hang out at the pool with the neighbors and we all became like family. We went to happy hours together, watched football and generally looked out for each other. I was fitting in nicely, drinking less, refraining from any drug use and overall feeling better about myself and my choices.

Johnny was spending every night at my apartment and I was enjoying the attention and company. He couldn't have been any nicer to me and anything I wanted, I got. We would visit the sights around Houston on the weekends. He was teaching me so much about life and things I hadn't even thought of. He was refreshing, genuine and down to earth. I remember thinking this must be what it feels like for someone to love you and I could see both of us falling for the other, while he captivated me with his kindness and generosity.

That first Christmas we were together, Johnny traveled to New York to be with his family. He left a set of keys with me so I could keep an eye on his place. Being the dutiful girlfriend, I had gone over and given it a much needed cleaning, top to bottom and I thought, "I wonder if he always lives with his place this dirty." I knew this was a red flag, however my instinct wasn't to run from it but to fix it, to take care of it, and I guess in a way, to overlook it since he had been so good to me. This was learned behavior, that if anyone does something for you, you owe them. I didn't know how to give or receive unconditionally.

We were missing each other, burning up the phone lines, and as a result, the charges. One day Johnny directed me to go in to his file cabinet, find his credit card, and use it to buy a ticket and come to New York. He said we would visit Niagara Falls and his college town of Oswego. I was so excited; I followed his instructions to a tee.

Being in love is one of the greatest gifts God could have ever given us. You feel butterflies in your stomach, excitement in the air and everything takes on a beauty of its own. When you are with that person, no matter where you are in the world, you are home. We were no different. The trip to New York that first year solidified our position as a couple, and we were no longer seen as two individuals merely dating.

Johnny was treating me like a princess, and every month on the day we met, during that first year, I would receive flowers. I was eating it up. He and I became the "it" couple in the complex, hosting parties and barbeques that were popular, I thought, *this must be what it feels like to be prom queen and king*. He even helped me buy my first *new* car, a 1989 Mustang.

I had gone from being abused to living a fairy tale. I finally felt respected and accepted by my family, not for anything I had done, but because Johnny was going to be an attorney. It was that or the fact that my life had settled down; I really wasn't sure, just glad to be fitting in. I seemed to really be growing up and filling that desire of mine to be good and do good.

There is an old saying *be careful what you wish for* because you acquire it and it does not live up to your expectations. What you thought would make you happy, does not. I was feeling overwhelmed by all this attention and affection he was showering on me. I dreamed my whole life about having someone love me, having someone want me, however knowing only rejection, I didn't know how to respond.

I was feeling smothered and as a result, about every three weeks I would ask Johnny if we could talk, and I would explain my feelings, requesting he stay at his apartment. After one night he was back at my place since setting boundaries was foreign and uncomfortable for me. By doing this though, I was starting to gather some confidence practicing this new grown up form of communication, talking about what was bothering me instead of screaming, yelling, and cussing. I hated hurting him, but for the first time in my life, I was trying to be honest about how I was feeling. All along, though, I carried the guilt of what the constant rejection had to be doing to Johnny, and thus, I could never keep the boundaries enforced. I was honing my people pleasing skills, myself and my needs lost.

At the same time I was practicing how to set boundaries, Johnny was taking up similar interests and we started going bike riding. On one of these junctures, I fell off a curb and broke my tail bone. I believe this is where my re-introduction to pharmaceuticals began. I had experiences with Valium on a few occasions, but this accident opened up a whole new world to me. I made a strong case to myself that they were legal, no more street drugs for me, telling myself, I was better than that. After all, Johnny was going to be an officer of the court and so began my justification. It started with the pain meds for the accident and progressed when I began using them for simple headaches and then any old ache and pain. Next, I would visit my doctor, explain the stress of working for my mom, and he began prescribing valium and before I knew it, I was using them all for family get-togethers or social events.

During the first couple of years I made myself believe we were an average couple, the relationship getting more serious as every month went by. One day I called my cousin and I asked her, "What should I do, I feel like he cares more for me than I do for him," feeling saddled with guilt.

Her advice still rings in my head. She said, "If you want to be happy, that is how it has to be." So we continued with Johnny trying hard to please, always looking the other way, and me questioning, "Should I stay or should I go?" while I did my best to minimize my drug use.

During the time we were getting to know each other better, Johnny had this way about him that I could see bothered some of my family. He was educated and appeared to be well versed in all kinds of subjects. He had this offensive habit though of shoving his point down your throat which I ignored because I believed he was so much better for me than my previous choices. I let Johnny have his way when it came to us staying together and he let me have my way in almost everything else. With this imbalance though, hostilities were brewing.

In fifteen months we went from living in separate apartments to moving in together in a two bedroom, two bath in the same complex. We also got engaged, twice. The first time we were drinking at the Hotel Galvez, swimming in the pool when Johnny got down on one knee, proposed and I said "yes." I didn't think it was fair though to say yes under the influence of alcohol and I didn't know if I meant it. I was afraid to go back in to marriage, and as a result, I had a hard talk with him and we remained single and unattached.

A few months later, Valentines day 1989, Johnny had an ad come out in the newspaper pledging his love for me, asking if I would be his. He met me in the parking lot of my dentist, newspaper in hand and as I exited, having just undergone a root canal, he asked me to marry him, roses and ring conveniently ready. I said yes and proceeded to put on his mother's ring and, to the best of my ability, wear it with honor.

My mother was very upset because she thought we were not ready, that I had gotten involved way too soon after Jamie. My stepdad even sat me down and warned me about professional students and I could see he was trying to protect me. They had my best interest in mind, but I completely ignored both of them, thinking I knew best. Once again, marriage seemed to be the natural order of things. Johnny put on the pressure, and I caved. All the while, this weakness of not speaking up for myself was escalating my drug use.

We began arguing early in the relationship and I can't recall when I first became aware of Johnny's rage, but I can remember the first time it brought me to my breaking point. Before that, our arguments ranged from his smothering to his need to be right all the time and of course, my drunken state at most of our parties. The resentment for not standing up for myself was building inside me and each day found me regretting the decision to stay in this relationship when early on I knew I had not wanted to. Feeling this anger towards myself gave me reason to take more pills, the cycle of abuse now in full swing.

It was late 1989 and I needed ankle surgery with a bone graft from my hip to correct a congenital condition. Once it was over and I was recuperating in our new apartment, all I could do is hobble from the bed to the bathroom with the aid of a walker. I was dependent on someone else for everything, and as the apartment became dirty, I asked Johnny to please clean up and do some laundry. He said he would. The next day, with the apartment still filthy, I asked him again and this time I could see he wasn't going to do it. He didn't move or acknowledge me. More anger, more pills.

I had flashbacks to his nasty apartment and started getting angry, not just at him, but at myself for allowing myself to ignore the red flag. While he screamed and yelled at me to shut up and not make a big deal about everything and just live with it, I cried, begging him to please clean up. The fight got so intense the neighbor upstairs had to come down to see if I was okay. I cried uncontrollably and as the argument intensified, crude remarks were made. It ended with Johnny leaving the apartment for a few hours while I sat on the edge of the bed trying to push the vacuum as best I could, one leg in a cast and stitches in my hip. I felt embarrassed and desperate, desperate for an answer to why was I so scared to leave him and desperate for a solution to the dilemma, do I stay or do I go?

I found some courage in spring, 1990 and began looking for a new apartment when the fighting escalated. I was going to leave Johnny and move out on my own. We had been arguing over everything and in front of everyone. It was humiliating and zapping all my energy. I had flashbacks of arguing with Jamie. I will admit at times I drank too much and I knew my dependence on the pills was in high gear, but instead of Johnny leaving me, he would argue with me and try to control it. I was miserable and I knew he must be too. I wanted him to have a little fun but he always resisted my idea of a good time. His kindness in the beginning, the fact that he was educated-the things that had drawn me to him were tearing us apart. And I wanted some excitement, I wanted my man to come in and laugh with me, joke with me, make me laugh. Johnny was becoming more of an authority figure to me instead of a mate and I felt judged all the time.

He was gearing up to graduate from South Texas College of Law in May while I put down a deposit on a new apartment and was getting ready to move. At the final hour, I froze from fear and my co-dependent nature forced me to stay.

I cried tears of relief at Johnny's graduation when the speaker talked about how hard it had been for the graduate's significant other. I thought, *finally someone who understands and is speaking out loud that he understands.* Someone was acknowledging my pain. My whole life it seemed no one had been able to validate my feelings and when this happened, I felt vindicated.

That one moment of confirmation by a stranger empowered me to believe there was hope for things to change now that the stress of school would be over. So we stayed together and we stayed engaged.

What happened next had to be some form of intervention. During this time in 1990, my prescription drug use was escalating as my self esteem was taking a dive. I began writing my own scripts for valium after taking a pad from my doctor. I happen to tell my sister's roommate about it. The ripple effect ended in my whole family knowing about it and my mom called my doctor. I admitted it to him, apologized, and went into my second psych hospital, this one focused on drug rehab. I spent about 30 days there and it worked, for awhile.

Getting out of the hospital was scary because everything had been taken care of for me. I was gearing up to go to Paris with my mom and I was excited, and looking forward to it. While on vacation we had a great time and I even attended twelve step meetings and was practicing sobriety. My mom was extremely supportive and I could tell she really wanted me to succeed. The trip allowed my heart to heal just a little, however the guilt I carried over being an addict and all that went with that was enormous.

Returning from a week in the city of love and lights, I was feeling very romantic. I missed Johnny terribly the whole week and wished he would've gone with me. Absence really did make the heart grow fonder. I had been sober almost two months and was feeling positive about the future. Upon returning home Johnny made a suggestion that we go down to the Justice of the Peace the following week and get married. It just so happened that the next week marked three years since our first encounter out at the pool that hot day. So three years after we met, on August 22, 1990 we married at the justice of the peace in Montgomery County, Texas, full of hope for a future together.

PHOTOS

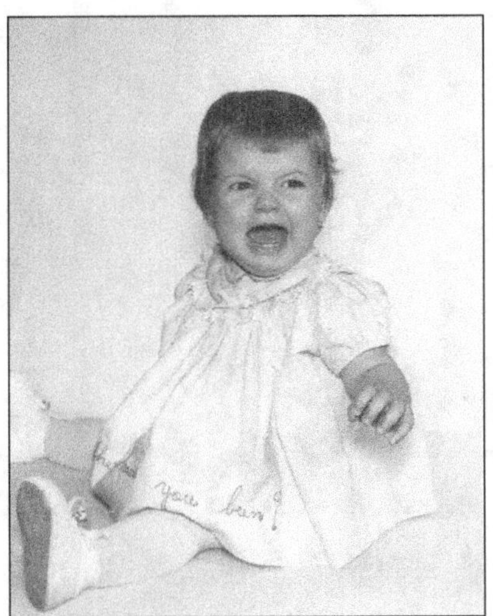

Not a happy camper, possibly an early premonition, 1961

One of the happy times with my dad, 1964,
when we first arrived in Houston

Us three girls, '62 or '63

First grade, 1966

With my older sister in front of our first house in Alief, 1969

My birthday, 1971, in love with Donny Osmond

The first true love of my life, 1977

With my BFF, 1978

Family together post Big D during the trial reconciliation, 1979

With Edward Van Halen at our first meeting, Houston 1979

Alex Van Halen and Michael Anthony with us, Houston 1979

Backstage with David Lee Roth, Houston 1980

Halloween, 1982

My nana and me, 1981

Mom and me, 1984

My first wedding, that day I thought it would last forever, 2-15-86

Second wedding, a little wiser, 8-22-90

In front of the White House, 1999

Times Square, 2001

In a sea of bluebonnets, 1998

Their first communions, 1998 and 2002, respectively

The pictures that carried me through many dark days (unframed)

On a vacation to NYC a few months before attack, 2001,
trade towers behind us

2005 right before custody battle began

September 24, 2006 getting baptized at Second Baptist by Dr. Young

Jordan's graduation, 2010

Christmas, 2011

Plaque hanging in my living room that says it all

CHAPTER 9

"When a prophet of the Lord is among you, I reveal myself to him in visions, I speak to him in dreams"

Numbers 12:6

STARTING OUT AS A MARRIED COUPLE, the atmosphere felt light and promising. Johnny had secured a job with a law office and was studying to take the bar exam. I had been sober for a couple of months, the fighting had lessened and our future seemed bright. Our friends had given us a honeymoon suite at one of the nicer hotels in Houston as a wedding present. We had a party there a couple of weeks after we got married and invited our friends to come and use the hotel pool with us. The room came with chocolate covered strawberries and champagne and before you could say honeymoon suite, I drank the champagne. I gave no thought to my sobriety while partying with our friends.

The decision to drink had come too easy. What happened to our romantic honeymoon? How had we let it turn into this free for all party? The only thought I had at the time was that I was married now and if Johnny was okay with it, then everyone else could go jump in a lake and that evening, he seemed to fully endorse it. Justification again.

Shortly after our marriage and seven years after taking the civil service exam, I landed a job at the Post Office, following in my father's footsteps. This almost doubled my salary from the current job I had, which made me feel like I was finally getting a break from life, and gave a much needed boost to my self esteem.

Johnny and I had been trying to have a baby and every month I would anxiously take a home pregnancy test and every month I would cry reading the negative results. I spent hours investigating why it can be difficult to get pregnant and found out that you should have your husband wear boxer shorts, so naturally, I bought Johnny new underwear. Everyone thought I was crazy and overreacting but I had silently carried so much shame and guilt since the abortion, I thought I might be punished forever by not conceiving again. I held everything in, always trying to present a good girl image.

At the same time in early 1991, some good friends of ours had a baby and we went to visit them at the hospital. Holding their baby boy, I fought back tears as I longed for a baby of my own. To this day I am not sure if it was the boxers or holding the new baby, but nine months later, one of my greatest accomplishments came in to this world, my girl, Jordan Rose, the most beautiful, perfect baby I have ever seen.

Being pregnant had agreed with me and I loved it. Feeling the baby inside me, I knew what a miracle I was carrying and I was grateful. I showed my gratitude by abstaining from any alcohol and drugs, however I overdosed on Mexican food. My girl arrived on November 25, 1991 at 11:41 pm all 8.06 lbs and 21 inches of her and she was magnificent. I was the happiest I have ever been in my life.

I had strayed from church after Big D, but managed to come back on my own a few years later around the age of twenty; however my attendance was sporadic. It seemed I always knew from a little girl that there was a power greater than myself. I used to lay in our front yard and through nature, feel God's presence. It seemed He was always calling me and trying to get my attention. My family used to make fun of me and say that I was too sensitive and deep, when all along I just knew someone or something was speaking to me.

Shortly after leaving Jamie, I started attending church by my new apartment, at St Francis de Sales and they assisted me with an annulment. Johnny, also being raised a catholic, started attending with me a few months later. We got involved, helping with the annual bazaars, attending bingo, meeting all kinds of people and making new friendships. Soon after having Jordan, we both felt strong that we should baptize her and since we had not obtained the church's blessing on our marriage, we decided to combine these. We had an awesome celebration; family came in from all over the country as we presented our daughter to the Lord and blessed our union. Life was good, even though I was hiding a little secret that would soon explode.

Shortly after Jordan's birth, I asked a friend of mine whose husband was showing signs of being over medicated, who and where his doctor was. She had confided to me while I was pregnant about her husband's condition, and that she felt his doctor was a quack. I explained with all the stress of being a new mom, trying to be perfect at everything, I was feeling overwhelmed and really needed some help. She reluctantly and with stern warning gave me his name and number and this set the ball rolling.

I was on leave from the post office and quickly realized I couldn't go back. While working there as a substitute carrier, I had learned what a lot of government workers already know, abuse of power. I showed up every day for work, minded my own business, followed every rule but still, everyday, no matter how hard I worked and how successful I was, the supervisor talked down to me like I was subhuman. She would also scream at me from across the station and it was humiliating. The abuse was heard by all and I was pushed to my limits.

After much consideration, reviewing my options, I knew I couldn't go back to the bank or to a job that paid so much less than the post office. Earning more money opened me up to a contrasting lifestyle and offered me hope for my future. I saw my financial struggles dissipate. Following a good deal of negotiations, Johnny and I agreed I would resign and go back to school. Johnny seemed to be the only person to date that encouraged me. After all the aptitude tests, I decided on the Respiratory Therapy program at Houston Community College for Health Sciences. Making that decision, I gained a fresh respect for myself.

By summer 1992, I began taking the prerequisites and refresher courses required while my visits to this doctor became more frequent, he prescribed Valium and Soma, a muscle relaxer that took me to never land. A pattern seemed to be developing of rewarding myself when the pressure of a big test or huge project was over. I was hiding my drug use well, or so I thought.

In the fall 1993, my last semester in respiratory school, I had a professor who appeared to be catching on to me. I was arriving late to clinicals, looking disheveled and acting somewhat dazed. I usually had a Soma hangover and even though I felt okay, I didn't look okay. He called me to his office one day, inquired about my behavior and I ended up in the program director's suite. She asked me about the charges.

"Are these accusations correct?" she asked, adding, "Are you showing up to clinicals disheveled?"

"I have a toddler. I'm a new mom, and I am constantly arguing at home with with my husband," I responded, always the negotiator. Just to make sure I got my point across, I added, "And at my age of thirty-one, it has been so hard going back to school," sure that all of what I was saying was true.

I watched closely and saw her eyes darting back and forth from him to me, and it appeared she didn't really know who to believe. I was hoping she would remember how we had become friends at the convention, taking tequila shots together.

I quickly interjected, hoping to push her to my side, "My grades are passing and I am managing the strain and I promise to manage it even better. You have my word."

My program director was convinced and let me off the hook. She dismissed his accusations as unfounded.

With that, I graduated in December 1993 as a certified respiratory therapy technician. I landed my first job and was offered sixteen dollars an hour. It appeared all the work of the last two years was paying off financially.

We were living in our first house, an 1100 square foot rental, owned by my mother. My drug use diminished that last semester of school after the intervention by my professor had me taking a hard look at myself. With the pressure of school off though, it was starting to gradually intensify. By late spring 1994, Johnny was tired of finding me intoxicated and moved out taking Jordan with him. I immediately retained the services of one of the best divorce attorneys in Houston and on the first hearing, I was granted custody. That evening Johnny came over to visit, had dinner with us, spent the night and withdrew his suit shortly after.

We tried to act as if everything was okay after our little court drama but it wasn't. We resumed fighting, I continued to use, and my job performance was affected. I had a wonderful boss; she was extremely supportive and in August 1994, she suggested drug rehabilitation and reassured me that my job was safe. That encouragement was what I needed at the time. The shame and guilt I continuously carried was causing intense harm and I was sinking so much deeper into regret and remorse, any confidence I had gained was waning.

I entered Bellaire General Hospital for the second time, the first when I was fifteen and spent two months there. This time I entered their RAPHA program, and remained twenty eight days.

During my stay at this christian based facility, I had a dream that was so profound. Its effects marked the beginning of my search for the truth, and although I was not fully aware of it, for God too. It would still take many more years for me to receive the fullness of it though.

In the dream, I was walking down this cobblestone road and Jesus was with me. He wasn't in front of me or behind me, but rather on the side of me and we were not talking, just walking. That was it. That was the whole dream, me and Jesus walking side by side. For someone who hardly ever dreams, this was very vivid and clear. The meaning I got was that he's *here* with me, he's my friend and he's helping me, guiding me, supporting me and loving me.

Johnny, in his fault finding way, pierced my self esteem just a tad bit more when he said, "I can't believe you think you are equal to Jesus!" as I verbalized this dream and my interpretation of it to him. Where I had desired and sometimes gained his support in the past, I now felt completely judged. This had become a pattern early on but his behavior seesawed. We had developed this sick cycle of abuse, he would scream horrible things in his rage and then feeling bad he would do or say anything to make it up, while I sulked silently, believing I deserved his cruel words and more. Afterward, I would numb myself to try and repel the offensiveness of his verbal attack, not wanting to accept the terrible things he was saying about me, the damage to my self esteem in full swing.

During my stay at Bellaire General Hospital in 1994, I met my psychiatrist, Dr. Thomas Brady and I will be forever grateful to God for sending this man into my life. Before this, whenever any of us would want or need therapy, my mother, who meant well, would send us to her friend, a psychotherapist. I loved this woman like a second mother but I believe it was impossible for her to be objective due to her friendship with my mom. I believe that skewed her perception and she could never empathize with me over the lack of nurturing and any other issue that had to do with my childhood.

Dr. Brady was the first professional that validated my feelings and helped me overcome many demons. With his help, I was able to let go of most of the anger toward my mom that I had carried for so long. I also gained much understanding about my parents and their relationship. They had done so much better than what they were raised with by giving us girls more material possessions; however, what we needed also, was love and affection, encouragement and confidence because they were just as essential. He even informed me of a time when my mother had called him to talk about my treatment and by telling me of her violation, he had built trust explaining the inappropriateness of her actions. Yes, Dr. Brady certainly had my best interest in mind and he was the first person to ever show me that without a motive.

Within a month of being discharged from the hospital, I became pregnant. Once again the happiness of being with child took over and there were no desires for substances. our months along we found out it was a boy and I was overjoyed, coming from a family of mostly women. My second greatest accomplishment came into this world at 1:21 pm on May 25, 1995. He arrived weighing 9lbs 12 ounces, was 22 inches long and we named him Matthew Steven. I was on top of the world and in love all over again.

At the same time, Johnny and I began seeing a Christian marriage counselor. I believe we both wanted our marriage to succeed and thus, we both committed to doing the work. We continued going for about a year and things got better. Most of the year though I was pregnant, and that meant for us, a happy and joyful time.

Shortly after Matthew arrived, the desire to use substances returned, but it appeared I had it under control. I was working part time on the evening shift, so the kids only had to go to the babysitter four hours a day, and only two to three days per week. The stress had lessened with this new schedule.

The following year I received a promotion at work and this newfound responsibility seemed to give my confidence a boost. I was working in a nursing home, managing the ventilator unit and in this environment, I was thriving. The employees and I became like family. The refreshing atmosphere helped kill the desire to numb that lifelong feeling of never fitting in. Being part of this "family" agreed with me. I was making friends and forming bonds that have lasted to this day. I was contributing to something that was much bigger than me and by helping the facility, my employees and all the patients, I was making a difference that was palpable.

With all the success I was achieving at work, things at home seemed to be settling down. Johnny and I were getting along and we were enjoying our children. I continued seeing Dr Brady and followed up with my therapy. Shortly after Matthews birth, we were planning his christening and I felt much stress. The desire to use returned. I lived with this feeling of not being good enough and that everything I did was being judged by everyone, but especially my family. I was still trying to fit in and knew that I did not. The desire didn't last long though and now it had taken a back seat to this new found confidence and outpouring of love that came as a result of my new position. I had people all around me who believed in me and supported me.

Over the next few years Johnny and I had some conflict with my family, but he and I managed to present the appearance of a strong unit in support of each other. On the rare occasions I was over-medicated, my mother would ask him what was wrong with me, and he would answer with "She's just tired."

We continued to fight but tried to give the appearance of a solid couple to friends and neighbors. Our same old argument over money and his position with the firm kept rearing its ugly head. I struggled with what I perceived as disrespect from his office that came from the way they treated him with the lack of salary they paid him. I was earning almost the same amount as he was with a one year certificate of completion. He had been with them almost five years and had not received one raise. At one point, my mother offered to put up one hundred thousand dollars for him to open his own practice and he declined. I couldn't understand why he didn't want better for our family. One of the final straws came when his bosses made the promise of partnership and then never made good on the commitment.

To make matters worse, if we didn't have enough stress already, around Easter, 1997, the four of us got sick, with Hepatitis A, and Johnny and I were out of work for two months each. A short time after we recovered, I began noticing I was having a lot of physical pain in my hips, back, and joints. I couldn't fight off a debilitating fatigue. Both of my sisters had auto immune disorders and I felt relieved that maybe I had somehow escaped their horror. After consulting with one of them to gain a better understanding about the illnesses and advice on how to diagnose them, I asked the doctor to draw blood and test the rheumatoid factor and SED rate, which measures inflammation in your body. Sadly, both came back abnormal, the rheumatoid factor positive and the SED rate elevated, thus came my diagnosis of Fibromyalgia over the next few months.

It was 1998 and I was thirty seven years old when I began seeing a rheumatologist. I was fortunate to find a great doctor because at that time most physicians did not believe it was a real disease. Fibromyalgia attacks primarily women in their prime and since they look normal, it was hard to accept, as well as to visualize the severe nature in which it manifests itself.

The next couple of years I felt like a human guinea pig, the doctor experimenting with every drug imaginable to try and get the disease under control. My moods were all over the place while I tried to comprehend that I would be "sick" forever, there being no cure for this ailment. The not knowing what was going to happen to me, to my family, to my children kept me in a certain amount of fear.

Prior to this, my health had been fairly good with only a little high blood pressure. It took years and much experimentation with a couple of different doctors to get the illness under control and manageable enough to live a somewhat normal life, and negotiate my own activities of daily living. Around this time, Johnny began videotaping me any time I was over medicated, gathering his ammunition. I was caught off guard while at the same time, attempting to manage two illnesses.

In 1999 we lost my stepfather and for the first time, I saw my mother altogether depressed. We all tried to rally beside her and lift her spirits but it would take time.

I will always give credit to my stepfather for helping my mother to soften. It appeared she had finally been able to receive the love that had been stolen from her own childhood and this began to change her. It enabled her to transmit that love back to her husband, to us, her girls, and in an unconditional manner, to her grandchildren.

While still grieving our loss, we rang in the new century and rested in the calm atmosphere as things had settled down, at least for awhile.

CHAPTER 10

I do not understand what I do. For what I want to do I do not do,
but what I hate I do

                               Romans 7:15

MY JOB HAD BEEN GOING WELL but in 2001 the facility decided to close down the vent unit. I had been approached about staying on in a regional capacity but declined. My answer was, "If you are kicking out my staff, I am going with them." At that time, I asked Johnny if I could take six months off for a much needed rest and he agreed.

During this time, I sunk into a deep depression, coming out of a job I loved for seven years where I had been respected, cared for, made lasting relationships and had a sense of self. It felt like defeat, but that wasn't an option since my mother raised me, repeatedly instructing about how we, as Italians, came from tough stock, so I soldiered on, suffering in silence, forever trying to wear that brave mask, and always denying my feelings.

The pressure I placed on myself to give the appearance of being perfect was immeasurable and extremely damning to my self-esteem while I learned to believe my own lies. I spent countless hours and endless amounts of energy masking my family's imperfections. I would brag about my children's activities, first with Jordan in dance, then both of them in t-ball and later swim team. I tried to depict the image of a perfect marriage with Johnny catering to my every whim, hiding the bullying and rage he presented at home, and as best I could, my little issue. I gave Oscar winning performances as he appeared to most to be the "nice guy". It was only family and a couple of close friends that could see more, read between the lines and knew something big was brewing. Suffering from a growing depression, I acted as my own doctor, diagnosing myself and over medicated much of the time, continuously trying to balance my illness of addiction with my illness of Fibromylagia.

Over the years I would go to twelve step meetings from time to time when our arguing would get really out of control, and things would calm down for awhile. I would always manage to stay sober for about sixty days and then something would divert my path, usually the sensation of things settling down and me reasoning, "I've got this under control." One of these times was when I went back to work in the Fall of 2001.

The summer had been eventful while we took a vacation to upstate New York to visit Johnny's family. I was over medicated a lot of the time, thus embarrassing and humiliating both of us. After arriving back home, I agreed to begin attending the twelve step meetings once more.

The school year had begun for the kids in August and just as they were settling in, September 11, 2001 happened and our country was under attack. I lost a cousin in one of the world trade towers and could not tear myself away from the TV that whole week. I was like countless other Americans, hoping against hope that we would find survivors.

I thought I lost my sobriety and used the attack as an excuse; when you're an addict, you will use any reason, good or bad, to feed the disease and acquire that euphoric state again. Clearly though, I was overcome with grief at the horrific events and Johnny compounded it by stating, "Why are you so upset? You didn't even know him."

It was partly true in the fact I hadn't met my cousin, but I knew his dad, not to mention we were close with all of our family in Jersey, so this painful statement pierced my heart. I was grieving like most of the country, not just for my family, but for the other three thousand that were murdered on that awful day.

Again, though, I permitted my dictator husband to tell me how I should feel and act, giving my real feelings a back seat to my life with no courage to speak up except in anger. Suffering in silence was becoming all too familiar.

My sabbatical from work ended and I returned, accepting a part time position. Filled with pride after maintaining, and then leaving a management position in the nursing home, I thought I was lowering myself to accept a floor therapist job, but I did it, after all our agreement was six months and we needed the money. After nine months at this new hospital, I was offered a position to fill in as relief supervisor while the real one went on maternity leave.

Soon after accepting my new role, I showed up inebriated and still high from the night before, after Johnny and I had a huge fight. I can't use our conflict as an excuse though, as many people argue and don't make the choice to self medicate. This clearly shows how lost I was and the behavior of an addict which was evidenced by this lack of moral choice. Given this new opportunity for a promotion at work, I never would have jeopardized my new position had I not been sick.

A coworker called my friend Raquel who worked for the same hospital and before we could attempt a counter strike, an administrator found out about the situation and got involved. She made me take a urine drug test, sent me home in a cab, and I was humiliated beyond belief.

My disease was fueled by denial, that denial whispering I had nothing to worry about, the medication was prescribed; however I was mortified at the turn of events that morning. The louder voice was that of reason and self protection convincing me to quit before they fired me and to take a hard look at myself, my life, and how I got to this place.

The old saying is that the road to hell is paved with good intentions and my experience has shown it to be true. When I resigned, Johnny and I sat down and had a long talk. I admitted I was aware of the severity of how out of control my dependence on pills had become. We decided that I would take a year off and with less stress, I could focus on attending a twelve step program and staying sober.

The humiliation I felt for years at not being able to maintain any length of sobriety had me convinced I was letting everyone down. My mother was so angry at me and let me know it with her episodes of disowning me. I was anchored in guilt and shame. Even I couldn't understand why, when I didn't want to take pills, I would anyway, knowing fully there would be consequences. I felt judged all the time by the two people I desperately tried to please, Johnny and my mother, and the more I was judged the more I sank into remorse.

My children, like most, demonstrated unconditional love. I believe, if not for them, I would have given up a long time ago. It broke my heart every time Johnny would videotape me with them present, and in anger, he would scream out, "Look at your mother, she's nothing but a f***ing drug addict". At this point in our marriage, Johnny had me convinced I was a bad mother and person, shoving it down my throat every chance he got from his pedestal. My next move would be the first in my walk towards wellness, but I would continue to stumble a little while longer.

The next year started out smooth and I settled into a routine, attending a twelve step meeting every day at noon. At first it was difficult because I didn't know anyone. I had found a new club to go to because my embarrassment over not being able to stay sober, kept me from the old one. Just the thought of facing the old group stirred anxiety in me.

Slowly, I started opening up, mostly to men since they were easier to talk to, but soon I found a female sponsor. I would sit in meetings, listen to all of them share and debate silently, *I am kind of like these people but not really, some of their stories have similarities but a lot of them do not.* As they spoke, it was easy to create any excuse to find myself unique so I could then ask, "What am I doing here?" I was clearly standing in judgment of my new found friends. While I pondered over Johnny and I being professionals, I found myself believing we were in a higher class and therefore better than the people sitting there.

I stayed sober for a few months, a first for me, until Spring 2003 at which time I found out Johnny had been hiding money. I happened to overhear him talking to his brother and he was instructing him on what to say about where he got the new camera from that Johnny was sending up. I confronted him and we were up all night while he confessed he was hiding thousands of dollars in an account at his office. An addict doesn't need much of a reason to use and live in drama, and this gave me a huge excuse to numb my pain.

Once the horror of the relapse was over, I continued on this path of sobriety, picking up a new desire chip. Around this same time, I consulted with an attorney, the same excellent one who had helped me in 1994, and inquired about a legal separation. I was keeping a journal and brought it in and showed her what had been going on in our household, especially with regards to the rage, mental, verbal and emotional abuse. She explained my options and shortly after my visit to her office, Johnny found out about it. After much screaming and crying, we had another heart to heart talk and decided we would work things out and both of us would destroy evidence we had on each other. Always the loyal one, I kept my word, but didn't find out until later, he had not kept his.

I continued meeting all kinds of characters, enjoying the meetings and the openness in which I could share my feelings. In August of 2003, after experiencing months of sober living, I was miserable at home because I was changing, but the fighting was escalating and I was having a hard time coping sober.

Johnny and I quickly saw that the peace agreement wasn't working and that we were continuing to argue over the same old things regarding his job and lack of speaking up for himself about the promise of being made partner. We also fought over what I perceived as his lack of ambition, his one raise in now almost ten years with the firm, our constant conflicts over parenting, my unwarranted insecurities and jealousy, and of course, my little problem.

Johnny believed in the old fashioned type of discipline like spanking with an emphasis on humiliation as he would make Matthew pull his pants down. I, on the other hand, believed in using time outs for consequences. At one point I jumped in front of our young son as he was crying, trying to undo his jeans getting ready for another whipping from Daddy, and I screamed, "You want to hit someone Mother F***er, hit me". At this point, it was horrible, the fighting, the yelling, the hitting and our language in front of the kids.

Without a strong foundation, no house can stand and this is true with people too. I had a few months of sobriety under my belt, but I had thirty years of making the wrong choice, and once again I took the path most familiar, in response to the constant fighting. After a very humiliating argument with Johnny, I buckled and endured an eight day relapse, of which I have basically no memory of.

I awoke in Methodist Sugar Land hospital with a nurse telling me I was going to be committed to West Oaks, a psychiatric facility. Quickly, I began to think of ways to work this situation to my benefit and being the master manipulator and consummate survivor, I agreed to admit myself, so in effect, I could discharge myself. There would be no one controlling me, or so I thought.

I can compare that first year in the twelve step program to winning small battles along the way.

As we would argue, I would take my new found tools and put them into play, ensuring the right choice a lot of the time, but I still couldn't hold up yet to the strain of a big war.

During my stay at West Oaks, I tried to listen in the groups, participate in exercises and truly open up about what was going on. I really wanted help.

"You can't come home," Johnny came up and announced one day.

"Where in the hell am I supposed to go?" I asked him.

"I don't know and I don't care, I am divorcing you and if

you do things my way, you can have unlimited access to the children," he said.

Shocked and hurt, I began to cry. Where was I supposed to go? What was going to happen to me? Didn't he love me anymore? Over and over these questions tortured my already exhausted mind.

I began to follow Johnny's lead but I can honestly say it never felt right. He had a hard time looking me in the eye as he spoke.

"You are the better parent right now, that's true. We should separate with you keeping the kids, and let's see if I can get well," I said to him, fully believing in what I was saying.

"We've never been apart so if this works, we can get back together," I also reminded him. "Think about the kids, forget about us, consider Matthew and Jordan, and give my idea a chance, please," I begged.

"No I am divorcing you," he reaffirmed.

I pleaded every day for three months and he never swayed.

I have never been so scared in my life. I listened to my husband though and he helped me rent one of those hotels by the week. That is where I stayed for the first half of a month. We would do things with the kids, and he would let me come over to the house and wash clothes. On our outings, he would hold my hand or put his arm around me and I thought things were going well.

One afternoon, about ten days in, he asked me to sign some legal papers, and told me once I did he would have the agreements changed to give me that "unlimited access" to my children. I asked him to let me read them first and he agreed. I will never, ever forget that exact moment and where I was standing when I read those horrid words..." You will stay 200 feet away from your children, you will not carry a gun around your children...."and the rest is a blur.

I sank down, the wall in the hallway the only thing holding me up, and as Johnny grabbed me to keep me from hitting the ground, the tears began rolling down my cheeks. Before I could say anything, he was trying to reassure me he would have things changed on the paperwork.

I couldn't fathom what would have made him get a restraining order on me and then violate his own order as we went go-cart riding and out to eat those first two weeks. I had never even owned a gun, and he certainly knew how much I loved my kids. I can't describe the shock I felt at reading that order telling me to stay 200 feet away from my own children. I had never hurt them or ever would, as a matter of fact, I was the one who didn't want HIM to hit them.

Most mothers would take a bullet for their children and I was no different. So I sank and fell and then fell apart, but not completely until I got back to the hotel. As a matter of fact, that had to be the first grown up thing I had done in a while, not fall apart in front of the kids. And I stayed sober through it, and that was definitely a first. I was heading down the right path and with no one trying to control me, I could finally keep a clear head.

CHAPTER 11

*I tell you that anyone who divorces his wife, except for marital
unfaithfulness, and marries another woman commits adultery*

Matthew 19:9

LEAVING 2003 AND ENTERING 2004, Johnny filed for divorce and the battle began. The last time he had been somewhat decent to me was that day in the hall of our home when he attempted to catch me as I slid into shock over the paperwork. Immediately following that incident and over the phone, he stated we were now adversaries because I would not sign his papers that he promised to have changed.

I was distraught but still did not envision Johnny as the enemy and I couldn't believe he saw me that way. I pondered the question, where had all the love gone or at least the love I thought we had? We had just taken a huge vacation to Hawaii nine months earlier with the kids, and by all appearances, we had a wonderful time. We also lost Johnny's father two months prior and I thought he must be grieving. We all were. *What's going on?* I kept asking myself, living in this passive aggressive, co-dependent relationship.

Johnny had transformed right before my very eyes into this split personality that, in sixteen years, I never saw. Whatever occurred between us, I didn't intentionally try to hurt him, only love him. At that point, the little confidence I had was destroyed, his voice repeatedly picking at the hideous scab that was my self esteem, inflicting more damage to the already open and bleeding wound. Little did I know, he was just getting started.

I obtained the services of that great attorney I used in the past and we started our counterattack. We filed a lawsuit of our own and began a plan of action. I endured about six weeks without seeing my children with the judge extending their protective and restraining order. Once we went to mediation, access was granted, but only under supervision. I was relieved to be able to see my children but dumbfounded as to what made Johnny lash out the way he did and why was he trying to punish me. It appeared he was playing God, and when I reviewed our history, I came to the conclusion that had always been his role.

During all of this, my mother had sided with Johnny and I didn't blame her. Everyone wanted me well, but no one thought it would happen. About two months in, after observing Johnny's ruthless attacks and seeing that I was staying sober, my mother quickly rallied behind me, giving me the encouragement I needed to fight.

At the same time, I had been going to meetings every day, sometimes two a day, and the club was becoming my home away from home. As far as my living arrangements, during the second week of my stay at the hotel, Johnny's attorney tried to have me served, and on the advice of my own lawyer, I avoided him with a few tricks of my own. My ex sister in law, Jamie's sister aided me in averting the server; it was a game of cat and mouse.

My attorney told me to go home, that I didn't have to leave just because Johnny said so and so I did. I unloaded the van of the few things I had with me, mostly clothes, and when Johnny got home, he wasn't thrilled to see me.

"What are you doing here?" he asked.

"I'm home," I summoned the courage to say, full of anxiety and hating confrontation.

"We'll see about that," came his sharp reply and he walked away grabbing his cell phone to call someone.

After a few cross words were exchanged, I called my attorney, couldn't reach her, and next I called my sponsor. Since I was in fear, she advised me to call the police. Once they arrived, Johnny pulled out his papers, the protective and restraining order, and they asked me to leave or be arrested.

Crushed, I loaded up the van, and on the way out, I grabbed a small 2x3 inch double wide frame with my kids' school picture, freezing the moment in time when our lives were forever changed.

The hardest part though was seeing my children, Johnny, some of the neighbors, and the cop witnessing my humiliation as I reloaded the van and backed out of the driveway. I held in the tears until I got around the corner, out of Matthew and Jordan's sight. I then fell apart, letting out a tortuous scream followed by more uncontrollable sobs, not knowing where to go or what to do. At that moment, on that awful day, my heart was ripped right out of my chest and I could feel the shift in energy. Until then, I still had hope.

I couldn't figure out why my lawyer would put me and my kids through that. She knew Johnny had those orders. I was quite dumb founded while I was being schooled in the games attorneys play, their ultimate goal, winning at any cost. Thus my disdain for lawyers grew even more.

I landed at the home of another new friend I met the previous year, a gay man named David, who was also in the program. I called my dad from David's backyard and through uncontrollable sobs, I unloaded everything on him.

"I hurt so bad, it feels like my heart is broken in a million pieces dad, and it will never be put back together," I blurted out.

"Honey, I know it does but you are strong, and you will get through this, I have faith in you," my dad tenderly answered as he tried to console the inconsolable.

It seemed odd to me, but once I was out of the toxic environment, I lost those strong, all consuming desires to use substances and fear seemed to be driving me and keeping me sober. Feeling relieved for the reprieve, I focused on dealing with Johnny's latest onslaught regarding the divorce and custody battle.

I was receiving all this support and encouragement from my new friends and was becoming part of their family. Even I was shocked as I picked up a thirty, sixty and then ninety day chip that marked the length of my sobriety; after all, I had never made it longer than sixty days in the past. It appeared circumstance had humbled me, my mind became open, my heart willing, and now, I could stop focusing on the differences between my new friends and me. It was very freeing.

The biggest game changer that I finally heard, was that I was sick and not a bad mom or person like I had been led to believe by Johnny, or making bad choices, which is what I heard from my family. Once that truth entered my psyche, an all consuming desire, not just to stay sober, but to get well had taken over and a big weight was lifted.

I complied with every court order and would cry myself to sleep each night, thanking God that I stayed sober that day, continuously praying for strength but missing my family. I honestly thought that this process would be fair and all I had to do was tell the truth.

I was feeling empty at the loss of my children, but accepted that no matter how I pleaded, Johnny was divorcing me. It felt like he was throwing me out with the trash. In November 2003, I rented a two bedroom apartment at the urging of my attorney and mother; they said I needed to show I could provide a home for the children. I was paying child support to Johnny, another diversion of his to try and make me lose my way, so for now the kids and I would have to share space since that was all I could afford.

With everything stacking up against me, I really needed to catch a break. My first miracle and clear indication that God was watching over me, guiding me and definitely had a plan for me was the fact that I was staying sober. The second was in my new apartment, through never ending tears, when I begged him to please take away the desire that I was carrying for Johnny. I couldn't sleep or eat, was pining away for a relationship that wasn't and hadn't been, if ever, working. On my knees, it was immediate, striking like lightning, coursing through me, and I felt the change. It happened so fast, in a millisecond, and even before I got up, I knew I had never experienced anything like that. God answered my prayer and mercifully removed that all consuming feeling that I couldn't live without my husband. With this supernatural act, I was assured that God and I picked up where we left off when I was a child and would commune with him through nature. It was nice to be back.

Early on, I could see Johnny's pride was going to put our

family through hell and nothing I could say would make him ease off and consider the children. Four months into this nightmare, at Christmas 2003, he took the children to New York to visit his family for the holidays. While there, I received a call from my daughter pleading and crying for me to please call her Daddy and make him get her help. She was having an asthma attack and couldn't breathe and told me Johnny wouldn't do anything. Feeling powerless, I called and received the typical Johnny treatment with him ramming down my throat that I knew nothing and was useless, so I resorted to begging him to call the kids' pediatrician and, at a minimal, get a rescue inhaler. I even asked for a pharmacy number and said I would call our doctor.

He kept dismissing me and arguing with me until finally, I could get a word in, and I rattled off the fact that asthma is the number one killer of children. I then warned him if anything should happen to our daughter, I would hold him accountable. I'm not sure what changed his mind, but I think I struck a nerve with my warning and the thought of how this could play out in court, and he made the call and got the medicine.

At the same time that life seemed to be falling apart for me, I was driven by hope that my newfound sobriety would afford me the peace and happiness that had so far eluded me in my life. I was extremely lonely, having gone from being a mom and wife to living by myself. Johnny was using the children as pawns by keeping them from me as much as he could. At one point we asked the court to allow my sponsor to be one of the people who supervised me and he fought it and won. However, he would allow my sister, still lost in her own addiction, to sit with us. It was obvious to most he was angry, lashing out, and trying to punish me. Proof was everywhere and I could sense it was the start of the biggest uphill challenge of my life.

To make matters worse, I was at the mercy of a judge who, entrusted to be impartial and fair, appointed to execute un-prejudiced rulings, and to enforce and render consequence for violating court mandates, was from the start, the exact opposite, appearing to favor the opposition.

Sitting in meetings every day, you tend to get up close and personal with the other people and eventually I met someone named Jesse who seemed to take a genuine interest in me and my huge problems. It was very easy to let him in since I was missing my children and had no where to release my energy.

It began innocently enough with Jesse, through a friend-ship first, and I found him usually consoling me as I had this tendency to cry my way through meetings the first few months. He would recount stories of his days in prison that he could connect to what I was going through, and it usually helped at the moment. He also had this vast knowledge about God and could move me with stories from the Bible, feeding the fierce hunger in me.

For some reason I was not scared off by his time in prison, but should have been as my attorney husband was using ev-ery trick he could come up with to make me look unfit, and I played right into his dirty hand. I honestly believed it would not harm me in court because this man was in recovery, seek-ing a better life, and from what I could see, appeared to know God and the way to Him. In my eyes, that was respectable and demonstrated good strong moral character and I believed I had nothing to worry about.

I quickly saw that I hadn't lost the ability to hear my inter-nal alarm but I did lose the power to trust myself, and therefore, adjust for it. I expect this confidence was forfeited through the destruction of my self esteem, if I ever had any to begin with. There were red flags from the start and I never heeded any of them, my desperation increasing.

On our first "date", we made arrangements to drive to Galveston to hear one of our comrades do her comedy routine. We set a time of 8pm for Jesse to be at my apartment so we could ride together. I bathed, dressed, and then waited.

Nine rolled around and I thought, *Where is he?* Around ten o'clock, I got undressed and in my pajamas. At ten fifteen or so, I received a call from the front gate and I didn't answer it, the first sane action on my part. He was pleading with me on the recorder to open the gate but I resisted. He left and about ten minutes later I got a call on my phone, and answered it. As I listened to his excuse I thought, *I have to cut this off right now and go no further with this guy if this is how he thinks he can treat me.* It wasn't just being late but the sorry reason he gave that he had promised another girl he would take her to a meeting, and he knew her longer than me, so she came first.

We argued over how inappropriate I thought this was and I questioned why he even made plans with me. At that precise moment, the tempo was set for our entire relationship, that being the first, but definitely not the last, where I can consciously remember going against my own intuition. Many more incidents like this would follow and each time, Jesse's behavior was like a whittler, chipping away any confidence I had.

One day, early on, we had just gotten out of a meeting and he went up to a girl and said, "You look so great today, you must have brought the sunshine out," with me standing right next to him. I asked myself, *Is he mentally challenged, why is he so inappropriate?* Every fiber in my body was saying walk, no, run away as fast as you can, but I wouldn't or couldn't as co-dependency had me frozen in fear.

While Johnny was busy scheming, I was trying to balance life. I had constant court appearances, my energy zapped from fighting to see my children, learning to trust this recovery process, working several jobs to meet all the financial demands, managing my health problems, and seeing to Jesse's every need and desire. It was exhausting. All the while, I believed I could take on more; after all, I was raised to be strong, and to always remember that Italian stock I came from.

One of my first indications the legal system wasn't working for me was the fact that the judge had extended Johnny's protective and restraining order early on. After that, it was one bad ruling after another, never in my favor. 2004 began with me being sanctioned five hundred dollars because Johnny said I didn't answer questions in a timely manner. Next, at six months sober, I cut my hair and had follicle tests done to show I was clean of drugs. I then asked the court to lift the supervision out of the visits with my kids, all to no avail.

When Johnny persuaded the judge to rule against me, I really considered he may be bribing him. Their tricks were never ending and as I paid an expert witness to testify for me, they rescheduled, a ploy to make me spend more money, always doing his best to break me. I was learning a lot about myself and my ability to survive.

Jesse continued to perform his high wire act, balancing his good guy image in public and covering up his deeds done in the dark. He was two people, relaxing at home but hitting the on switch whenever we went out, and it was one of our biggest arguments. I couldn't listen to Avril Lavigne sing, *Complicated,* without being reminded of him. For everything Jesse did wrong, though, he did one thing very, very right as he ushered me in to God's presence in a way, that I believe, no one else could have.

CHAPTER 12

Blessed is the man who perseveres under trial, because when he has stood the test, he will receive the crown of life that God has promised to those who love him

James 1:12

AT THE END OF 2004, I was still questioning how unfair this process seemed, and I kept asking myself, was it the system or the judge, as most of his rulings were against me. I couldn't catch a break which led me to think Johnny must have this judge in his back pocket, but reality kicked in and I knew he didn't have that much power. He was angry all right, but we had no real money, at least not the kind it would take to bribe a judge. It wasn't until after we finalized everything that I found newspaper articles revealing accusations of impartiality toward females, and alleged failure to hold attorneys to court mandates, proving it was the judge who had been unjust. Until then though, I, along with my friends and family, were left to speculate.

I requested the court modify our temporary orders, offering

up proof through witnesses that the kids were being left unsupervised, in unsafe conditions and with no food. The neighbors were calling and informing me they would show up at their homes, hungry, asking to be fed. They were also in dangerous situations when left alone, one time climbing on the roof of our home as reported by the next door neighbors. Another incident required a 911 call for an injury my son sustained and he was hospitalized. I sat dumbstruck as the judge did nothing.

In addition, Johnny was court ordered not to take me off the health insurance or let it lapse and once again, the judge looked the other way as Johnny grossly violated this order, leaving me with no coverage. I was continuing to cut my hair, more follicle testing being done, proving I was sober, and he continued to rule against me. There was order after order, never in my favor.

At that same time, I switched attorneys, a decision I would later question, but at the time it appeared to be the right thing to do. My original lawyer had not been answering my calls the entire summer or moving quickly enough. She also admitted to me upon the first follicle test, that she didn't believe I was sober until the results came in, proving to her that I was. I needed someone in my corner, believing in me because I didn't know how to trust or believe in myself yet. It didn't appear that she was fighting hard enough, ignoring my calls, and this time away from my children was killing all three of us. I needed someone to fight for us, and that justification was all I needed to fire her.

In December, after hiring the new attorney, we reached a Rule 11 agreement which finally lifted the supervised visits, sixteen months after they began. The stress and damage the restriction put on my kids and myself, is still being undone today, our wounds healing slowly.

Entering 2005, another motion was entered as I attempted

to expose more of Johnny's disregard for the mandates. He had liquidated our frozen retirement account, and again, the judge turned a blind eye. It was never ending with all the unfairness.

At one point I tried to make amends, pleading, "Johnny, I am so sorry for my addiction, for the trouble my actions caused, I never meant to hurt you," believing my words might help him to let go of some of the anger.

"I don't care," came his sharp response followed by "It's a little late for apologies, Fran, they're meaningless now."

I heard Johnny's voice in my head, reminding me I deserved this and more but I thought I would try one more time so I asked, "How can we expect to be forgiven by God if we don't forgive?"

"God may forgive you, but I don't," came his stoic answer, "I never will."

He was out to destroy me out of some sort of sick revenge and everyone could see it so I had to walk in God's forgiveness, covered by His grace.

During all of this I was managing to keep busy with my attention diverted to my new relationship, while also trying to map out a life for myself. Early on, Jesse and I had a lot of fun together but for all the joy, the misery was doubled. We could not go anywhere without having a conflict, and it was usually with me trying to control him because he was aroused by someone or something else.

About a year after we met, I took him to San Antonio for his birthday, and we stayed at the historic Menger Hotel. I wanted to treat him for the support he was showing me through this court battle. We went out to eat on the Riverwalk and to a club to go dancing. The entire night at the club, Jesse found a provocatively dressed woman to obsess over, ignoring me and the conversation I was trying to maintain with him. Once I picked up on what he was doing, I stormed out of the club, and he came after me.

I screamed at him, "Why? What is wrong with you? Why aren't I enough for you?"

Like a dog with his tail between his leg, he apologized after admitting fault. His words cut through me as he said, "I don't know why, she got my attention and I couldn't stop, I am so sorry."

We had many incidents like this, just different location and different girls.

When I met Jesse I was beginning to feel good about myself, and the fact that I was changing my life for the better. My self esteem was climbing and I was learning to take care of myself, enjoying bubble baths and time to relax. The sheer fact of staying sober was a much needed boost to my confidence.

After I began seeing him, this all changed as we became closer and learned more about each other. He had this male chauvinistic side, very controlling, demanding his way in everything from the kind of bread we ate to what we did on the weekends. In the evening, he would come over after work and I would make these home cooked meals, beginning with a beautiful salad, served up with hot bread right out of the oven. Instead of being grateful someone was cooking for him, he began to degrade me with, "Why don't you cook like my mom did?" "Don't you want to make what I like?"

In my eager to please state, I put so much pressure on myself to fit the mold he wanted. I was constantly trying to change by losing weight, fixing my hair different, buying new clothes, paying for dinners or nights out, and planning getaways, but it was never enough. I couldn't hold his attention and by staying with him, I destroyed what little confidence I had. I often wondered why he didn't walk away as it was obvious he wasn't satisfied with me. I believe he was as weak as I was.

During all of this, the main driving force that kept me hanging on was that Jesse had this unbelievable knowledge about God that I had never seen or heard before. He fed this hunger in me by sharing hours upon hours in my little apartment with stories out of the Bible and I couldn't get enough. I knew "of" God and had shared a closeness as a little girl through nature, but I didn't "know" God and therefore didn't have a personal relationship with Him. Lacking this, I didn't know how to let Him take care of me or place any reliance on Him.

Jesse had a unique manner of responding to that need and by listening, observing, and inquiring, he helped me carve out my own direction I wanted my spiritual life to go in. He also had this knack of relating God's truth to our own lives and circumstance, and our twelve step program using comparisons. It was exactly what I needed at the time to feel comforted and feed this all consuming desire in me.

He helped open my heart by saying yes to my request to pray together and no man had ever done this with me. This established a bond I never knew could exist between a man and a woman as you bring God in. He also turned me on to Christian rock music which helped open my spiritual side or consciousness in a way that only music can.

I was a little girl when God and I lost that intimate connection, around the time of Big D, and Jesse helped reunite us. I took all this interest in me as proof that he really cared and loved me. I kept telling myself that if I was patient, he would grow and eventually let go of his sick need for attention from others and his lusting after women. I was in major denial and it would take a violent implosion for me to come to my senses since I ignored all the red flags along the way.

For all the negative in our relationship, he had an uncanny way of provoking laughter, at the time, a much needed medicine. My feelings for him went very deep, and as I was losing everything, Jesse in his finite wisdom, knew how to direct me to the only one who could give me hope, God. For that I will be eternally grateful.

While Jesse and I were trying to fall in love, I continuously dodged bullets from Johnny. I was followed by a private investigator, and generally treated as if I had no rights. I was bullied at every turn, and through all of this, it was hard not to believe Johnny, who was constantly saying that I deserved it. However I had a mother, a program and a God who were telling me different.

My mother had come out of retirement a few months prior and was working part time in Florida. She would fly in to almost every hearing I had and be at my side. This is the time, through all of this turmoil, that we really became close. Throughout this ordeal, I witnessed the love that only a mother can have for her child and I finally understood what Dr. Brady had tried to show me about her. She had always done the best she could and by her support now, I knew her love was genuine. I could tell she wanted what was best for me and my children, and I loved her for it.

As we entered the summer of 2005, we were asking the court to confer with the children, and not surprisingly, the judge ignored our request. Around that same time, we asked for a motion to compel discovery and for sanctions and it was denied. There was motion after motion, games played on both sides to delay or try and sway the case to their side, and all to no avail for us.

Johnny and his team were winning and had been winning from the start. All those years of taping me, strategically placing our children in the videos, calling the ambulance any time he could and firing off accusations to anyone that would listen were now paying off for him. He definitely looked like the big tough guy and succeeded in making me appear to be "bad". A bad mother, a bad wife, a bad person, you name it and Johnny was basking in it.

I had always believed Johnny when he said he didn't lie and had bragged to others about his honesty, but my big lesson in this was that we all lie. He lied to get what he wanted. He lied when we said we would destroy evidence we had on each other and try to make our marriage work. He lied when he hid money from me and he lied as he gave some to a family member behind my back. He lied when he told the court he paid for his attorney as he had early on confessed to my sister and mother that his representation was pro-bono. He lied about the price we paid for our home. And he lied for years to my mother about my little problem.

My saving grace was that deep down I could feel there was some good in me. I was a woman of integrity. I knew my intentions were good and honorable. I knew I never meant harm to anyone, even though I saw that my actions did at times. I knew that if I gave you my word, I followed through. I knew I wanted the best for all people. And I knew deep down I was an eternal optimist. I had been sick with this addiction, wandering around lost in my life, looking for happiness and meaning, and taught by society that marriage and children would bring it. Now I was re-evaluating everything. As I found the road to recovery, I was grateful and could see I had much to look forward to as well as much work to do.

The thing I held on to was hope. Hope that if I stayed this new course, things would be different for me and anything had to be better than the misery I had been living most of my life. And I had hope that even though this judge had shown favoritism, I still would get a fair trial. I needed to have something to believe in.

Proceedings began on our fifteen year anniversary, August 22, 2005. As the trial went on, I could see early on that things were not going well for me. I had absolutely no control over anything and it felt horrible. Witnesses were called, accusations made, and proof offered up, and even though it was more than two years old, it was usually very damning towards me.

Finally I was put on the stand around eleven thirty one morning, and as my furor over the last two years rose, I took on an aggressive and aggravated tone with Johnny's lawyer. I began by responding to him using his first name, and the judge quickly corrected me and ordered me to address him as mister. Unable to conceal my anger and frustration any longer, I succumbed to their game and lost my cool.

After only thirty minutes of my testimony, we broke for lunch, and immediately upon returning, the judge called the attorneys in to his chambers and gave them an ultimatum. He said he was tired of it all and this is the way we have to settle things. Johnny would get everything, the kids, the home, child support and even our Texan football tickets. Our retirement was gone and no one bothered to bring it up again, probably because the first time we did, we were ignored. He said Johnny would also acquire the debt we had, when added up, was about twenty five thousand dollars.

The judge gave another ultimatum too. He said if we did not agree to this, he would make it worse for me, pinning the entire debt on me in addition to the child support which, was going to more than double now. Feeling the threat, I began to mentally review the last three months.

During the trial, I held on but it got hard as I endured ruling after ruling, never in my favor. One day through cross examination of Johnny, my attorney was apparently having personal problems and cried through the entire cross. I was horrified, but somehow soldiered on, a forced compassion for whatever she must be going through helped me stay calm.

On another occasion, Johnny's lawyer had my mother thrown out of court because she was a witness, but she had already testified so this was their way of trying to control and maintain momentum. The judge again allowed this injustice to continue. All day she sat on this cold, hard, cushion less bench in the hall of this very old Wharton, Texas courthouse, that strong Italian stock shining through, nothing rocking her foundation. I was so glad she was my mother while I watched her set an example of strength and grace for all of us.

Another day Johnny showed up with a front tooth missing, was on the witness stand, and looked out at me, directly addressing me with, "Yeah, I'm missing a tooth." I looked at the judge, then my attorney and back to Johnny and, feeling embarrassed for him thought, *What am I supposed to say?* He then looked at the judge and said again, "I'm missing a tooth". It was surreal, like I was in some kind of serious courtroom drama, with a comedic twist, and uncanny timing.

During all of this I was complaining to my attorney about the unfairness of how we were asked to split our material possessions with Johnny having all the power. I was angry that my requests for Johnny to copy pictures and video for me, continued to be denied or outright ignored. He acted as if I didn't exist, wasn't the children's mother and he wouldn't allow me to step inside our home any time I picked up the kids. This had started early in the separation, right after I wouldn't sign his papers he promised to have changed. He had complete control, and a cocky swagger of authority.

Feeling powerless, I decided to sneak into the house and retrieve my children's baby boxes, the one thing that mattered most to me in the world, the birth records and keepsakes of my children that I put together, not him.

As I nervously opened the never locked back door, I was reminded all those years ago when I had broken in to my neighbors house as a young teen. Once again I felt like a criminal, except now I was in my own home, and had an agenda that I believe any other mother could understand. It wasn't for money, or jewels or furs, not that we had any, but it was for the memories of my two darlings I brought into this world, something that could never be replaced.

I was stopped dead in my tracks as I entered the living room, tip toeing, a loud blast of an alarm went off. I thought, *Oh My God, someone is here!* I yelled out, in case it was his girlfriend, and in the event she may have a gun, "It's Fran, I'm coming in!" To my relief, it was an alarm clock that just happened to go off at the most inopportune time, almost scaring the nerve right out of me, my hair standing straight on end. I was already in though, on a definite mission to regain some control, and out, in all of maybe two minutes. As I drove away in triumphant victory, my eyes welled with tears, and I realized I finally scored one for my team!

I didn't get personal belongings out of my home, but rather "junk" out of the garage on the day we were allowed to come over and retrieve what Johnny would let me have through the division of property. I kept wondering, why did he have all the power? Where was the fairness in this? But then I remembered, none of this had been fair. The only moment of truth that day was when Jesse hit the house on accident with the U-Haul truck, as my mother laughingly whispered to him, "Do it again." Present and in my corner, I could see her trying to maintain some kind of control too.

The last day of trial, when we "settled" everything according to the judge's wishes, I stood on the steps of the courthouse, and while my eyes traced the outline of every car in the parking lot, I went to a really deep place within myself. I thought about everything that had occurred over the last two plus years, while I also reviewed my whole life. I contemplated, *It is all over now, all eyes will be off you, so go ahead and go out tonight and get as loaded as you want, he won, no one will care.* Immediately, not one second later, it was followed up by, *Or you can keep walking in this new direction and see what God has for you. You've been doing the other your whole life and what has it gotten you?* Immediately I knew I wanted to keep on this new journey, however I still had a one-two punch to go.

CHAPTER 13

"Go stand in the temple courts," he said, "and tell the people the full message of this new life."

ACTS 5:20

WITH THE TRIAL BEHIND ME, I knew life was going to be challenging. I was strapped financially, working four jobs at one point, all of them part time, as I tried to maintain insurance on the kids and myself, and keep up with the child support. With visitation every other weekend and one night a week, I fell into the tortuous trap that Fathers all over the country experience as you work hard entertaining your own children since your time is extremely limited. It is exhausting, not to mention the toll it takes on your pocketbook and whatever I did, it was never enough-enough time with them, enough money to spend on them or enough of myself left to try and have an impact on their lives.

There was so much guilt associated with this divorce and custody battle. My kids were suffering and it was evident in their demeanor, appearance and the frequent meetings I had with the school counselor. She wanted to come testify but the district would not permit it. It was frustrating because I didn't have the control, Johnny did, and he wasn't talking to me, or, trying to work with me. He definitely wasn't putting the children's welfare first, only his need to control the financial outcome. I wanted to do everything in my power to help my children but my hands were tied, and so I tried to lead by example and trust God that he would see us through and act in our best interest. I was definitely being schooled in patience.

With the support I received from my new friends in recovery, I knew I may have lost the court battle but was winning in the fight of my life. As Summer 2006 came around, I celebrated three years sober. My mother, aunt and kids had come to my two year birthday and this year I would invite my dad. My parents both spoke openly at the celebrations to the gathered crowd, stating how proud they were of me and grateful for the program that helped save their daughter. I was definitely walking in God's grace.

One day while getting ready for work, my children called me up, their voices frantic and full of anxiety. Before I could say anything, my daughter said, "Mom please come get us, now!"

After we arrived back at my home, they told me that they wanted to come live with me. They said that their father and his new family were not getting along with the two of them. They laid out a myriad of reasons and I listened closely, intent on trying to decide if, first, they were rational and second, did we even have a chance. I tried to stay calm and listen, recognizing we were all finally finding some ease in our new roles. I asked myself, *did I want to upset the little bit of peace we have,* trying to do what was best for my kids, but they were grounded in their decision.

I hired an attorney, produced a retainer with money I didn't have, and obtained a court date. Jordan, being old enough, had signed her affidavit expressing her preference to live with me. On the appointed day Johnny represented himself, and all I remember is the same judge, the one I couldn't ever catch a break from, saying, "Motion Denied."

Stunned, I later found out he used some law which stated orders could not be modified if it hadn't been a year since finalizing everything. I really went in believing my daughter, stating her choice, had given us a real shot. When this occurred, my distrust for attorneys grew even more and I considered that my own lawyer should have known this. Defeated again, I retreated, all too familiar with that position whenever I left his court, but nonetheless trying to reassure my kids.

During all of this I was attempting to nurture a relationship with Jesse, and I found myself exhausted as I tried to meet his every need. It was like having a third child, only this one I was granted full custody of, his needs and tantrums never ending. Me, in my intense need to control something, did my best to control Jesse, however it was a losing battle that was weakening every area of my being.

We had this terrible habit of breaking up, causing intense drama, and after maybe two or three weeks, getting back together. Every time seemed like the last for me, it was heart wrenching and never got easier. If his insatiable need for attention wasn't bad enough, his lustful way of always finding a new girl to start hanging out with, was. Each occurrence crushed my self esteem and any confidence I had managed to build; however, I always returned for more of the same, critically ill with co-dependency.

Jesse had a hard time staying sober and with each relapse, he sank further into the all consuming guilt and remorse that comes as a result. Through all of the constant disruption to our lives, it appeared he must have always returned to me as a sort of saving grace, since I was staying sober. It was something to hold onto, a way of staying near the light and away from the darkness. I remained with open and waiting arms, ready to accept just about any behavior he could dish out. Living in this insanity, being a doormat of sorts, I always believed each time would be different, fervently praying for him and the relationship to be Godlike. It never was.

Being stripped of my identity as wife and mother, I blindly basked in my newfound role as Jesse's savior. I stood on my judgmental pedestal, monitoring his activity and trying to break his code of secrecy that grew bigger with each passing day. I justified my position, speculating on his time in prison, fully believing that not only had I improved his world but transformed it as well with my light filled, God driven path. I was oblivious to my own pretentious persona which was in full swing, never admitting to myself or even realizing the depth of my grandeur delusion, not to mention the lavish buffet I was providing to my undernourished ego.

Shortly after we began dating, Jesse brought me to church services at a Baptist church. Being raised a Catholic, I tried to hide this from my mother, nonetheless I couldn't hide the positive impact it was having on me and my life. My spirit had been starved and I was now receiving divine manna straight from God. It became evident in the way I began to change and form a new belief system.

My living arrangements started to change often around this time. At the beginning of trial in August 2005, fully expecting to be granted my home, I discontinued my apartment lease, and signed a month to month at a much higher cost. That didn't happen and brought a whole new meaning to.....*do you want to make God laugh.*

In December 2005, after the trial ended, Jesse convinced me to move in with him and his nephew, to take a break from the financial strain and stress the last few months had produced. Feeling zapped of most of my energy, I reluctantly agreed. I was uncomfortable having my children come visit me there, forever changing the sleeping arrangements, as Jesse and I both agreed the children should not witness us in the same bed without being married.

Within two months, I went out and rented a two bedroom town home in my urgency to escape the awkwardness living with two men can bring. However, on the rare occasions when Jesse showed genuine concern for me, I knew his heart was in the right place in his attempt to remove some of my burden. It was these moments that I clung to, always desiring more, and forever coming up short.

At the beginning of 2006, I began attending church regularly. My heart gently opened every Sunday morning while I listened to the music first, and then absorbed Dr. Young's message, always the Word of God applied to today's inconvenient world. It took a while but I started to believe I was a perfect child of God, made in His image. I began to really understand the magnitude of what God did by sending Jesus to help us reunite. I had been lost but now I was found, just as the song says. And above all my heart was mending at the outpouring of love that God was showering on me. I left with a sense of peace that overflowed from me, and became acutely aware that I was daughter of the King and I relished this spot.

I was working nights and living in the town home. Jesse had followed me there at the urging of his nephew. It didn't last long though as one of his relapses saw him breaking rule number one, no drugs in the house. And so our second attempt at living together lasted less time than the first, about one month.

While living there, I had a routine I followed every day while getting ready for work in which I would have on the Trinity Broadcast Network (TBN) and listen while dressing. I was trying to absorb some kind of spirituality via osmosis, but mostly hungering for the Word of God finding Sundays weren't enough to fill my insatiable appetite.

One day a pastor caught my attention as he was asking the audience to give money to one of their local churches. I stopped and listened closely and he was talking about tithing, a word I had never heard before. When I repeated it, it seemed awkward to say and felt like I had a lisp. He captured my attention with the fact that he didn't ask me to send my money to him or to the TV channel, as I was a huge skeptic, extremely secular, and like most people, prejudiced to believe most television preachers just wanted your money. On this day though, I listened, intent on making my own choice, mindful of false prophets.

Shortly after, I read Malachi where it is written, test him in this, and so I decided to do just that. At the time, I was still working two jobs, paying child support and struggling financially. I was driving an old 1999 Ford Minivan, with a driver window that didn't work anymore, a/c had to be recharged every 2 to 3 weeks, and the gas to fill it up was extremely costly. Still, I decided to do what it said in Malachi and test God, thus, I began giving ten percent of my income to the church I attended.

I was attempting to move the kids and myself out of the town home we had been renting when my financial miracles began. For three years we had shared space, never having enough money for each of us to have our own room, so I was looking for somewhere with three bedrooms. I began looking at houses in the neighborhood where my children had grown up. Most of them wanted first and last month rent with a deposit and I didn't have it. One day I was driving by this old beat up house with dead, overgrown grass in the front yard and saw a "For Rent" sign. I saw workers there so I stopped, went in, and asked if I could look around.

I saw what I wanted to see, beautiful hardwood floors in about half the home, new carpet in the rest, shiny appliances right out of their packaging and a fresh paint job. It appeared to be a fixer upper and here were crews doing just that. I don't know what it was about that little neglected house, but a subconscious bond had formed between us, I had fallen in love and had to have it. The only problem now was that I needed twelve hundred dollars for the deposit.

Around this time the kids and I went to see my dad, in east Texas. They had not seen their Grandpa since before Johnny and I separated so we were looking forward to the trip. Upon our arrival, my dad escorted us in to his office and handed me an envelope. He instructed me to keep it between him and me and said no one else should know. I sensed it was money yet I didn't open it until that night when we went out to eat. Nodding at Jordan while I excused myself to the ladies' room, she read my cue, got up and followed me. Together, we crowded in a stall, my number one girl at my side, and trembled with excitement as we rapidly counted out twenty hundred dollar bills, unable to contain our joy! Instantly I knew it came from my heavenly Father through my earthly father, and finally, I had the deposit.

When we arrived home, I made the call and wrote the check. Shortly after, in August 2006, we moved in and I was elated to now be providing each child with a room of their own. The only obstacle I could envision now was that I didn't make enough to afford twelve hundred every month; never one to be defeated, I made a plan.

Upon returning home from visiting my dad, I had put the other eight hundred into a savings account that already had three hundred in it. I decided that this money could supplement my income, and we could make it through three or four months. I rationalized that if nothing changed, I would just have to get a roommate. There went the idea of each child having their own room but I justified that scenario was months away.

My next miracle happened soon after, but before I reveal it, let me say a funny thing about God. He seems to wait until the last minute, forever testing my patience or ability to withstand the given circumstance or trial, and then boom, he comes through, and I can exhale. With each test, trust grew stronger, and I no longer needed to hold my breath and wait for the other shoe to drop.

It was a typical day in October of 2006, and I was preparing to go to work. My daughter called and asked, "Mommy, do you remember what we've been talking about?"

Annoyed at her evasive nature and rushed to prepare for work, I said sharply, "What is it honey, Just spit it out!"

"Mommy, I did it, I am coming to live with you and Daddy said it is okay," she blurted out excitedly.

My reaction was involuntary. As I fell to my knees, listening to her words, I gave much deserved thanks to God for another miracle. I indeed was astounded.

Within a few days, she had moved in and two weeks later, Johnny and I came to an agreement that the child support would end effective November 1, solidifying my faith in God's ability to move mountains.

As happy as I was, I couldn't deny this nagging feeling in the pit of my stomach, echoing through my mind, *one down and one to go*, as division still lay between my son and I. Gnawing at me too was the fact that he and his sister would be apart now. For the time being though, I had to find comfort in this grace.

My tithing produced one financial victory after another. Every time I would receive a raise, I increased my tithe. I tithed before I paid rent. I learned one of my first valuable lessons that God was true to his word and I could begin placing my financial dependence on him. It was a relief to finally have some help.

The year 2006 was a memorable year during which I received many lessons as I began to grow and heal. I also joined as an official member of my church in August and made a public stand for Jesus, getting baptized a month later, on Sept. 24, 2006.

On the other side of the coin, I was still struggling in my relationship with Jesse. As 2007 came around, our saga continued.

CHAPTER 14

Submit yourselves, then, to God. Resist the devil and he will flee from you

James 4:7

I WAS ATTEMPTING TO BUILD a new life for myself and began walking with a certain confidence as I was letting go of years of shame, the longer I stayed sober. I was also processing a good deal of childhood and early adult dysfunction, healing slowly through the twelve steps. Finding my church helped satisfy much longing in me, feeding the Word of God directly to my under nourished spirit.

Although my new found walk in sobriety was agreeing with me, my relationship with Johnny was not recovering. He had agreed Jordan could come live with me, but I found out that was because his new wife wanted her out of the house to try and stop the violent arguments that kept occurring. For me, that was just fine, I would take her any way I could get her.

Johnny would not take my calls whenever I tried to reach him to talk about anything with the kids. Soon I stopped trying unless it was an urgent matter, and sadly, those too ended up unanswered and unresolved.

On the flip side my relationship with Jesse could only be labeled dysfunction junction. He had his own agenda and I had mine. As much as I tried to communicate, believing talking is the healthy way to resolve conflict and express desires, it fell on deaf ears. Resentments built as I would verbalize needs and he did nothing to ever try and meet them. I walked on egg shells, the turmoil constant between him and my daughter. It was a nonstop tug of war with me in the middle and I wasn't escaping unscathed.

The club had become my home away from home; we made many friends there, and the only problem was that it had turned from a place where we recovered to a social hangout. Unfortunately the place I was supposed to get healthy had become unhealthy. It was similar to being back in high school with all the different groups, the jocks, the nerds, the popular and unpopular. Jesse and I had been labeled the governor and Mrs. of the Delta club. As a result, whenever I had to share about my relationship with Jesse, I sugar coated everything concerning us and suffered in silence. By this time in my life, I had perfected *dressing it up*!

Around this time the sponsor I had been working with for three years stopped talking to me or taking my calls. No explanation, no reason why, all communication just ceased. I had placed calls to her asking what was wrong but they went unanswered. I would see her at the club and she would just walk past me as if I didn't exist. I racked my brain trying to figure out what I did to deserve this. At this point I wasn't healthy enough to rebuke the lie, so I accepted responsibility that I must have done something to merit this behavior. Living in this familiar role of being the victim, I felt abandoned, again, and I was crushed.

Not knowing how to support my new self esteem, I found it taking a beating every time I turned the other cheek to Jesse's latest antic, Johnny's erratic behavior or my sponsor's abandonment. My walk with God was my saving grace. No matter what happened, I could feel his love and light shining through. I started memorizing my favorite scriptures and creating a file in my mind that I could go to when needed. I began listening and attending everything I could and on January 26, 2007 I went to see a pastor I watched on TBN, Dr. Creflo Dollar. My invitation to Jesse was declined so I went alone.

Dr. Dollar caught my attention with his usage and interpretation of the Word of God. I had many judgments in the beginning, one being on his last name. After all, they are asking for money to support their ministry, and Dollar is his last name. I laughed but also stood corrected as I read his bio.

As I entered the George R. Brown convention center, journal in hand, the music caught my attention first. Boom, boom, boom went the pounding bass as it pulsated in synch with my heart. Any moment I thought it was going to leap out of my chest. Where were the nerves coming from? I reasoned that it must be from the newness of the experience and the fact I was alone.

As I looked around, I saw that most everyone appeared to be African American. Quieting any fear that may want to surface, I quickly reminded myself, "Relax, after all, you have more black girlfriends than white ones." But deep down I knew it went way back, back to the rape. Ever since that happened to me, I have had an apprehension around black males because the man Jamie had befriended, so long ago, was black.

Being alone it was easier to find a seat closer to the front and once I did, I saw that everyone was up, clapping, dancing and praising God to the music. I was raised in a very conservative Catholic church where the priest has all the power and everything you do is extremely ritualistic, so I was very out of my element. Even the Baptist church I was attending could be very conservative, with no one yelling out or displaying signs the Holy Spirit was moving them. We all sat in our seats, hands folded in our lap, in control, and silently in fear others might stare and think we weren't perfect.

However, always one to love music and especially dancing, I felt one hip involuntarily begin to move, looked down and thought, *what's going on.* Shockingly and completely out of my control, the other hip started jutting back and forth, and before you knew it, I opened up and allowed the spirit in me to worship God in a way I had never experienced before. It was indescribable, the powerful amount of love I felt that night from a room full of strangers, coming together with one thing on their mind, praising a God who loves and gives us that same opportunity. It was awesome. I prayed with people all around me throughout the night, learned much from Dr. Dollar and since, have gone back any time he is in Houston. My spirit was being fed and, as a result, part of me was coming alive.

Reviewing my notes from that night, a couple things stood out. I learned that God gave Adam, a man, dominion over the earth, and that the devil came illegally and stole that dominion, sometimes referred to as the keys, in the Garden of Eden. The only way to get them back was for a man to come, and get them back from hell. The reason it was illegal for the devil, is because God gave man dominion and man has to be of and from the earth, and the devil is not. Enter Jesus, born a man with a birth certificate, who was tempted yet never sinned, and when he died, went to hell and got the keys back, saving us all.

No one had explained it this way, ever. Of course I am giving you a short version, but it also explained where Jesus was for the three days after the crucifixion and for me, it was as if a light bulb had come on. I felt empowered just by having the knowledge.

In addition, Dr. Dollar posed a question to us in regards to the part in Genesis when God says, Let us create man in our own image, Dr. Dollar asked, "Who is God up there talking to?" and I thought, *I don't know, who is he talking to?* When he said it was Jesus and the Holy Spirit, and that they had been there from the beginning, I almost fell off my chair. Why didn't I know this? Why hadn't anyone ever taught this to me or pointed this out? Was everyone else in the dark?

I had just turned forty six years old, been to Catholic Church my whole life and no one had ever encouraged me to read the Bible, nor did it seem important to anyone. I realized I had an abundance of questions and decided to focus on the Word of God, discovering the answers I needed seemed to be there. What I found was so much more as every step I took towards God, he opened my heart and mind a little more and I could feel his love, and the empowerment I was gaining from obtaining this knowledge.

During all of this I had been working nights while my mother was coming over and staying to care for Jordan. However, I needed to switch to days and the only way my job could offer a position was to transfer me to a different location which was a lot farther away. Needing this, I agreed.

My first day at this job is the day I took ICU and the day that changed me forever. Realizing that it was the judge's son in the critical care unit that first day, my initial reaction was shock.

I completed my assignment in a zombie like trance while shaking my head in disbelief. That was the day my eyes were opened and I saw the mighty hand of God, up close and personal. I had been learning about Him, reading the Word and forming my own intimacy and relationship with Him, slowly learning to love and trust. But on this day, if I had any doubt at all, about any of it, it was wiped away forever, and I saw that God was in control of all things. I fervently prayed for the judge's son during this time I cared for him.

Around this same time, Matthew decided he too wanted to live with me and we began a project to make that happen. I went out and hired another attorney which cost another retainer I didn't have. I was not looking forward to this after my track record with the courts and lawyers. My previous experience left little hope in the back of my mind after what had happened when Jordan signed her affidavit; however, we filed and received a court date.

About a week before the hearing, my son conveyed a strong desire to stay with his father.

He said, "Mom, if I leave, Daddy will be all by himself and I can't leave him alone with those people," referring to his step-family.

He had already spent about eight months living with me and I could see he was torn, so I replied, "Things are fine the way they are, and if you want to stay with Dad, then you should."

I reminded him, "We have joint custody anyway, and you can come to my house any time you want to." I knew my son was having a war with his conscience and as much as I wanted him with me, I knew I had to make it easy on him with as little guilt as possible.

All I wanted is for both of my kids to be healthy, happy and thrive. I believe it is what any parent wants who truly love their children. He and my daughter had not asked for this difficult situation and all I could do was remember when I was that little twelve year old, not wanting my own parents divorce. Thus my heart ached every time I saw them in distress. And it ached with the remembrance that there was no one to soothe my own pain during Big D.

Throughout this entire tragedy, I kept comparing the similarities between my parents divorce and mine, viewing my children's innocence and ensuring that their emotional needs were met. I knew all too well what happens when they are not. And as much as I tried to do the right thing during the separation and after the divorce was final, I didn't always win. I wasn't always successful at stopping myself from letting my anger get the best of me and saying something derogatory about Johnny in front of them. But I saw the growth later on, and as I could recognize it, I went back and told them I was wrong and apologized.

By the end of Summer 2007 when the lease was up, I had moved out of the little neglected rental after the landlord did not hold good on his promise to fix some of the things that needed repair. I found a larger home with four bedrooms right down the street, maybe two blocks away, rent still the same. It was perfect.

I began to benefit more and more from the tithing, getting one job after another, and God being true to his word, each one paid more than the last. I left the hospital in just enough time to see the judge's son off, silently hoping God was proud of the love I had displayed towards him and his mother. Once I left, I realized the only reason I had worked there was to witness this demonstration of God's amazing power. There is no other way to explain the miracle of the boy and me meeting, and the opportunity God gave us all for healing to take place. The judge's son was with us about six weeks and I was there seven, and it was just enough time for divine lessons.

There is a saying most Christians know, and it is *you can't out give God*. As 2007 began, I was working for the hospital bearing witness to God's strength, and making about $42,000.00 a year. Upon leaving there and returning to a pulmonary rehab clinic, in a director capacity, I negotiated my salary at $60,000.00 a year. I was always a little concerned about my paycheck since this was a small operation, a kind of mom and pop company.

Four months later, one of the local hospital chains expressed interest and offered me a management position at one of their facilities. I really wanted to take it, feeling it was safer to have a big company behind my paycheck than a smaller organization. However, after passing all of my interviews, they offered me $63,000.00, two thousand less than I put down for minimal salary.

When the call came and they offered me the job, part of me wanted to take it, knowing it was still $3000.00 more than I was making, but a bigger part of me said to myself, "Why do they think I would take less money?" By now walking in fear was all too common and standing up for myself too uncommon, but I turned it down because I didn't want to sell myself short, a first in believing in me. I know God honored that belief because they called back a couple hours later and offered $65,000.00 PLUS a ten percent bonus paid out quarterly, contingent on the hospital making budget. I was deliriously happy, and could definitely see God's hand in all of this. Yes, Malachi was right, test him in this; all the while I continued to tithe. If making this much money was outrageous, then what happens next is an exorbitant display of God honoring His word.

I was still driving the old 1999 Ford Minivan that was really on its last leg, however me being the sentimental fool I am, I couldn't get rid of it. After all, it had seen me through the toughest of times, and the church was helping me maintain it through a single parent ministry. Etched in my memory is how I drove off from my house that day so long ago, waited until I was around the corner, and in my indescribable pain, cried out while I was forced to leave my children behind. Oh how this van had seen some stuff, but mostly, better days.

Shortly after accepting the management position, my mother had offered to buy me a new car. Immediately, like with the money from my dad, I knew this was from my Heavenly Father, and that my needs were more than being met. I was grateful that I had parents who would listen to their hearts.

On Halloween 2007 I picked up my new vehicle, and was extremely grateful, grateful for so many things but especially that I had a mother who tried to make my life easier. I took this as proof, proof that she cared, proof of her love and proof that she had always loved me. We too were healing through unspoken words.

I was finally beginning to trust that things were going to be okay, but I still had a few more mountains to climb.

CHAPTER 15

If they have escaped the corruption of the world by knowing our Lord and Savior Jesus Christ and are again entangled in it and overcome, they are worse off at the end than they were at the beginning

2 Peter 2:20

ENTERING 2008, JESSE AND I got engaged over the holidays, shortly after one of our famous break ups. This one was unusual only in the fact that it was I who did the breaking, but true to the pattern we already set, we never stayed apart. This time he came back full force, ring in hand, and he had it planned out, down to the waiter taking pictures of him on bended knee. Since he had chronic back problems, I couldn't help but ask if his back had gone out again as I watched him begin to kneel, but then sat speechless as I saw him dig deep to find the courage to ask me to marry him. And what I will always remember, is not that he asked me, but that he was able to let go of the fear long enough to get the deed done.

While Jesse and I were busy trying to maintain our relationship, the kids and I were trying to map out a new norm as things settled down. I was encouraging Jordan to find a job and learn responsibility. She began driving in November and needed her own money for gas and essentials. The year before though, we were still walking in chaos when my mom took us on a vacation to Disney, I saw my daughter's anger and it was directed at me through verbal assaults. I also witnessed my mother defend me and point out how I loved them, by fighting for them, and finally getting well for them.

Around this time I began taking my daughter to counseling, provided through my church and while Mom was continuing to help, Jesse was more of a hindrance. He and Jordan were nonstop at each others throats, it appeared always in some form of tug a war over me and my attention. And Jesse was forever going to get his way, but Jordan, God Bless her, wasn't going down without a fight. And me, forever in my critical co-dependent state, made one poor choice after another, feeling like I couldn't do anything right. If I took Jesse's side, we had peace but I carried a certain amount of guilt and if I took Jordan's side, I had no peace, only fear-fear Jesse wouldn't love me and fear he would leave me. So I attempted to just pick what I felt was the right thing to do in each situation, but forever doubting most of my decisions. This continued to chip away at any confidence I had left.

I was settling into my new job with the understanding that if I was successful starting up their respiratory department, we would duplicate it at the other nine hospitals. Prior to hiring me for this purpose, the corporation had contracted pulmonary services. With the help of my old boss who hired me, we amazed even ourselves with the great job we did, the money we saved the company, and the positive feedback we received from patients, families and physicians. By 2008, I was making a positive impression with the CEO and corporate office as a direct result of my perfectionism, and it was evident by the way my department was shining.

As summer rolled around, my landlord decided they wanted to sell their home. The husband was sick and needed a transplant. We began to haggle over the price and immediately, God said to me through prayer, "Do not argue over price, give them what they want, they need to be by their family." I was new in my walk with God, I was learning to let go of fear and control, and this proved to be another lesson in trust and obedience as I gave them their asking price. On November 24, 2008, I closed on my house and felt secure knowing no one was able to kick me out of my home again.

Jesse and I tried again to live together during 2008 but this time it lasted all of two months. This was the third time and it never seemed to work out. That alone should have told us something, only we were so enmeshed in such an unhealthy way, no one could have told us anything. I'm sure they tried.

In 2009 I began to worry about a problem Jesse and I created. I had begun sharing my pain medicine with him in 2005 or 2006 after some intense persuasion on his part about how much his back hurt. He told me how his brother had to go to the media just to get him another mattress when he was locked up. I told him if his back was that bad he should go to the VA and have some tests run. He did and got on the same medicine I had to take for my auto immune disorder. At first it was not a problem, but as time went on and years went by, he would run out, and I would share, which made me fall short and he had to share, and thus, by 2009, the insanity was in full swing.

At work, we lost our great CEO in September of 2008 and the whole hospital was devastated. By January of 2009 the new one had begun and no one could have predicted how much of a challenge some of us were going to face. Instantly he began humiliating me and insulting me at will in front of a room full of my peers. Being new at the corporate game, I suffered in silence with each incident pulling more of my self esteem apart.

In the spring of 2009, Jesse fell into another relapse that was worse than any other. I found him using drugs at my house and shortly after, he was fired from his job, after getting lost in East Texas in the company van. I carried much guilt because I thought if only I had never given in and let him have that first pain pill, he wouldn't be in this predicament, but my twelve step friends quickly pointed out that I didn't hold that much power. Needless to say, when the relapse occurred, fear engulfed him and quickly helped me to see that I had to step back, in order to help him. It didn't last long though, and I wouldn't technically call it a break up, just a break.

Through a family member, Jesse was able to secure a position as a distributor, with an up and coming energy drink so he wasn't out of work for long. It felt like a blessing for him to find gainful employment so quickly and we had no idea what ruthlessness lie ahead. We only thought we had troubles before; this experience gave me a new meaning to *hitting an all time low*.

The new job took Jesse into a world so sinister that I prayed for things to return to the former, and what I believed to be, the lesser of the two evils. I watched his ego grow and strengthen, while also feeding off the nightclubs, the events, the girls, the lack of clothes on the girls, and the BS that these kinds of sales people tell each other to get what they want. If I thought our past was torturous with Jesse's insecurities and womanizing, I was living in the fullness of it and I was miserable.

I prayed and journaled for God to help me detach with love

and for Him to reveal truth to me. I coped by telling myself he didn't sleep with any of them. And the bottom line is that I believed Jesse, who was a pro at coming up with excuses and justifying his actions and/or whereabouts. I sunk so far as to tell myself that my suffering was for a bigger reason, for God, my own ego supported off this lie as I fell into the all too familiar victim role and suffered from the martyr syndrome. It was so much easier to show people his defects than look at my own.

I continued to pray, attend church services and diligently seek God through all the chaos around me. I was in tears, distraught and could feel my insides being ripped apart every single day. I began to lose weight and got dangerously thin. I was so baffled because I kept thinking that this man, who helped me find this wonderful, loving God, a God who loved me just as I am, was a walking contradiction. And if having problems with Jesse wasn't hard enough, work was falling apart too. There was my CEO with his big mouth and insults, and to make matters worse my corporate level boss was laid off. She was the one who had hired me back after so many years to help her achieve this greatness and we had accomplished so much more. We had become the darlings of the corporation, for a season. Every morning I would get on my knees and pray. Prayer truly was my saving grace, and daily, God would sustain me.

Still trying to fit in at work and also do something I enjoyed, I joined the softball team, and began attending practices. I was desperate to map out a life for myself and could easily see Jesse did not want to be part of it. His ego had transported him to a whole new level, one that his elevator didn't stop at for us little folks.

I started going to a support group after reading up on co-dependency, finally accepting I fit the very sad description. I wanted so badly to get well now that I had acknowledged my co-dependent nature. As I pulled further away, Jesse did not fit the stereotype of opposites attracting. Instead of missing me and moving closer, he also moved further away.

One day in August 2009, I was talking to Jesse on the phone and we said our good byes. As always, I waited to hear the click before I hit end. I did not hear his disconnect so I proceeded to listen in, for an hour and a half.

I muted my phone, intent on hearing every word. I began to think about what I was doing, but that didn't stop me from eavesdropping. It took awhile for him to get to his office, but once there, I got an earful, and the shock of my life. I knew Jesse had low self esteem and suffered from the same thing I did, co-dependency. As a matter of fact, I had been so busy looking at his, I almost missed my own, but nothing could have prepared me for what I was about to hear.

I quietly listened while the man I loved dogged me out to his new boss, and if I didn't hear it myself, I never would have believed it. He sounded like someone I didn't know, and someone who was certainly not in love with me. He used slangs and spoke like a teenage punk.

"I don't tell Fran anything we do; I shut her down. She doesn't like the whole sex concept so I just shut her down," he declared, very matter of fact.

"I started messing with her five to six years ago," he said, talking about our relationship.

"This last time when I started messing with her," I heard him say referring to getting back together after one of our infamous break ups. He sounded more like a sixteen year old thug than a forty eight year old educated man.

I could hear his boss ask a question but couldn't make it out when Jesse replied, "She saw you with Amy, then Karen and she saw Carey's partner Susie and she saw all these beautiful women and they were all so young."

He was laughing out loud; laughing at me.

Where did this come from?, I wondered. I talked with all of the people he mentioned, I even hung out with Carey and Susie at one of the functions. Karen even joked with me about almost buying the same dress I had on at one club. And I never had a problem with my age, or tried to hide it like some women did. I worked out, took care of myself and felt proud of how I looked. As a matter of fact, it was Jesse who was sensitive about how old he was, which was six weeks older than me. I was dumbfounded and could see it was he who was controlling the friends I had, here at his job and at Delta, with his lies.

Jesse then said to his boss, "I told her too bad if you don't like it, I am going. I make her stay away," laughing, sounding somewhat diabolical, and addressing the club scene.

"Three times a week and then I spend weekends over there. Oh yeah, she loves it, she loves it," I heard him say, making reference to coming over my house, which was followed by more laughing.

"We will have the legit one with the spouses and then secretly, let's have the real one, the glow girl party," he blurted out, referring to the Christmas party and the models' nickname.

Most of the conversation I could not make out what his boss was saying, but towards the end, I heard Jesse tell him, "Fran's ex Johnny, he'll come at me one day, I am sure of it. I have to be careful because he'll take me to court to try and get money; he's a lawyer," he said in a braggart tone. But first, I admitted to myself, they had to make some.

At that moment, hearing him rant to this man like he was some big shot, I thought, *who is this? Who talks like this? Who tries so hard to put on an act for someone?* He had said he loved my children and he couldn't even say their name, referring to them as "the boy" and "the girl." And me, he told me every day he loved me, every day he prayed with me, and to hear him humiliate me like that, well that certainly wasn't any kind of love that I had ever seen or heard about. I should have known from my experience with Johnny that no one is who you think they are, but not getting the lesson the first time was costing me now.

After the infamous phone call, I left town distraught and went to see my dad in east Texas. Every day Jesse called, apologized and asked if we could work things out. After a week I came back and said yes we could.

I returned to Houston just in time for my sixth sober birthday party at the Delta club and Jesse showed up that night, and officially broke up with me. In shock, I was left wondering, *Why did he beg me to work things out? Was this some kind of game to him?* I dug deep to get through that night and cried through my entire speech.

We stayed apart almost two months, longer than we ever had, but as history had already proven, we couldn't stay that way. By Halloween, we were again going full speed ahead. God was revealing truth to me alright, although it was falling on deaf ears and I had more pain yet to go.

CHAPTER 16

The Shepherd leaves the ninety-nine and rescues the one lost... the hero isn't the sheep for repenting but the shepherd for getting the lost sheep... the sheep merely rests on the strong shoulders of the shepherd... the sheep receives the grace.....

Joseph Prince, pastor

2010 STARTED OFF UNEVENTFUL, and as we brought in the New Year, I had high hopes for my future, always the optimist and sadly, more often at the time, out of touch with reality. After the shock of my first sponsor's rejection, I found a new one in 2007 and we seemed to work well together, and with her guidance, I was sponsoring a couple of women myself.

My job was stable, but the humiliation I was suffering at the hands of the CEO was beginning to take its toll on me. I was leaving meetings in tears, after the horror of his outbursts. Things like, "Look at her, isn't she pitiful?" were spoken in front of my co-workers. Early on he made inappropriate sexual comments, but I ignored them. At the same time they stopped, the cruel ones began. But soon he began making advances through text messaging so I started documenting them, regretting I didn't do the same with the others. I hadn't put it together that this was his way of retaliating against my rejection, but once I did, I was safeguarding my position.

Jordan was working a part time job that she loved and finishing high school. Matthew was continuing to travel back and forth from Johnny's house to mine. We all were enjoying the most peace we had known since the separation in 2003 and, even though Johnny and I were not speaking, this was the most civil we had been. The only fighting that was going on now was between Jesse and Jordan, and it was brutal and never ending.

Jesse was continuing to work with the energy drink company, slowly inching his way back into his old job, since he had not received a paycheck from this man the whole time he had been working for him. He and I decided we would have a Superbowl party and invite our friends. Because we had limited space, I knew we couldn't invite everyone so we agreed on the guest list and omitted some. Behind my back he was secretly texting one of the women I was sponsoring, apologizing and asking her if she was okay since she hadn't been invited. I only found this out after the fact when she brought it up to me, thanking me for being concerned. She thought I had told him to do it. Even with the distractions though, the party went off without a hitch; everyone seemed to enjoy it and it was a huge success.

After suffering much humiliation at work, I was contemplating quitting my job, realizing I could only take so much. The problems with the CEO were affecting other co-workers that were attempting to climb the corporate ladder. They either jumped on his bandwagon and went along with his cruel little game, or said nothing but distanced themselves in order to protect their own job. We were experiencing lay offs and the atmosphere had been tense for months. As a result, I began to feel the anxiety, chaos and rejection all around me, and sunk into a depression, fully accepting I needed to make a move, but frozen in fear and unable to act.

In my critical, people pleasing state, I wanted to be accepted and liked by all, and this all too familiar rejection from my peers hurt. I decided to speak with a corporate level director that I had become friends with, and he appeared to be genuinely interested and reassuring concerning the CEO. After our talk, I decided to wait and see if things would get any better, all the while praying about it and everything else that was going on in my life, and learning through trial and error how to trust God.

I was standing in my bedroom when I got the call from my boss, a woman I admired tremendously, and she told me our CEO had been fired. This was the second time I involuntarily fell to my knees. A tremendous relief flooded over me like a tidal wave, and through grateful tears, I thanked God for taking care of the problem.

Going back to work and knowing the stress of being ridiculed would now be over, there was a sense of relief that was short lived. On Monday, March 29, 2010 I received a phone call that brought me again to my knees. It was my stepmother and she said my dad hadn't woken up that morning and she had to call 911. She said he was brought to the hospital and then life flighted to a bigger hospital in Tyler, and before I could digest the information she had given me, she called me back and said the doctor came in and said to tell me to come up and say goodbye.

Goodbye? What happened? Where was my dad going? Tears blurred my vision, and the reality of what she was saying punched me in the stomach, knocking the breath right out of me.

When the call came in, I was getting in my car, heading out to a doctor appointment, and as I hung up the phone, instinct took over, and I found myself beating the hell out of the steering wheel and dash, crying out, "Why God, why?"

I sat numb as my sister, the kids, Jesse and I drove to east Texas that evening and arrived at the hospital at midnight. It felt surreal, like I was in another world as I walked through the lobby, up the elevator and arrived in ICU. I did my best to transmit as much love as I could to my dad, holding his hand, my sister on the other side, and as we turned off life support, the spirit in me took over and I sang God's praises, thanking him for sparing suffering.

One of the hardest things I have ever had to do was write my dad's obituary, reeling from the shock, and full of sadness and anger-anger that he was gone too soon, with out goodbyes and anger at a stepmother who had done her best to shield him from all who cared about him. Sadness was for the overall loss. I would never have another conversation with him, or an opportunity to say I love you once more, and hug him or feel him hug me back. My dad hadn't always been there for me, but I knew he loved me by the way he spoke to me with kindness, a reassuring tone to his voice and softness in his embrace.

Inconsolable, I turned to sleeping pills that week, insurance against nightmares. At the doctor appointment the day I learned about my dad, I had asked for them, fearing sleepless nights from anticipated stress. Planning for disaster, I was creating my own.

Arriving home, I could not turn off the sadness. The world was closing in and I had many regrets. I saw rejection all around me and now my rock was gone. The one person that I could call and talk things over with was gone. The only man in my life who was consistent, was gone.

The other man in my life, Jesse, always seemed to let me down. Forever chasing someone or something else, rejecting and taking me for granted. I was suffering and usually in silence. In my critical co-dependent state, paralyzed by fear, I could not walk away.

All this sadness lingered like a bad smell, and I had to get rid of it and thus began the craziness. I began taking the sleeping pills morning, noon and night. A couple of friends tried to talk to me, but I wasn't having any of it. I wanted to sleep and didn't want to wake up. I didn't want to think and I didn't want to feel. I was sick of living in the insanity with Jesse and angry at myself that I wouldn't walk away. I tethered myself to the unfortunate victim role, bating the line with the pills and dangling it before my very nose like candy, and I was unable to differentiate the truth from the lies.

Two weeks later, very early in the morning, my cousin called and I started to open up to him. We talked about the way we were raised, the family dysfunction and how we both had struggled with drugs. We also spoke of God and how much He means to both of us, how His love covers a multitude of ailments, and in a moment of clarity, I knew right then and there I had to stop taking the pills or die. Wanting to live, I called my sister and made arrangements to meet my whole family in Las Vegas the next day, and in Sin City, this girl sobered up, again.

Jesse disappeared as soon as we got back to Houston, and I didn't hear from him or see him. I heard he was sleeping with the woman I was sponsoring, the one he had been caught texting two months before. They had been spotted together late at night, at the Delta club, laying together on top of his truck, hiding behind a refrigerator with clothes disheveled and the final one, making out in the dark in one of our meeting rooms when someone popped open the door. Six weeks later I received an email from him saying goodbye, it was over.

There is a saying, *it takes what it takes*, and in my case, it took this horrendous event to shock me into reality. It was the accumulation of years of unhappiness plus losing my dad that had me taking a hard look at my life. My dad died very depressed, married to a woman for almost thirty years that he wasn't in love with. He and I had conversations where I asked him if he still loved my mom and he always said yes. I thought, *I don't want to be thirty years with Jesse, and be this unhappy, there has to be more to life than this.*

Immediately I knew what I had to do. I knew I had to relinquish all rights to be an active member of my recovery group; however I didn't know how hard it was going to be. Everything inside me screamed, "Do you really think it will be different if you go back to Delta?" History had already shown me that when we broke up, we never stayed broken up. As soon as we were around each other again, some sick affinity for each other had us right back in the others arms and beds. I knew to break this cycle I would have to be the grown up and sacrifice and therefore, I gave up my friends and complete support system, the Delta Club. I told myself I could attend a new club, make new friends but that is easier said than done. I was feeling the huge loss from my dad, the loss of my group and now the loss of the relationship. Heaved on top of all this loss was betrayal. I was completely broken.

I walked around heavyhearted, grieving my dad, shocked at the audacity of Jesse and unable to let go of the shame of relapsing after almost seven years sober. At work, it was suggested I take time off to finish grieving and I welcomed the reprieve.

Once back, the promotion I was to get before my dad passed seemed a little too big now and I didn't think I could handle managing two hospitals. They agreed.

As hard as it was, I put one foot in front of the other and for the first few weeks, cried every single day. I was in shock over Jesse and his cheating. Prior to this, I knew he had a compulsion of flirting with girls, always giving the impression he was single, while he would introduce me to men as his fiancé, but to the girls as Fran. I rationalized that it was his low self esteem, always telling myself he didn't sleep with them. I thought with patience God was going to change his heart and grant him the desire for me and ability to be a good mate. And I believed him when he said that he just wanted to be there for the newcomer. I quickly saw that I had been living in denial.

Daily there was the obsession to pick at my scab, reopen the wound, and I couldn't stop focusing on what he did. Finally, a friend suggested a therapist and said, "If you've ever done one thing for yourself, go now and get help." I did, and every Friday for six months, I was in his office, talking, listening, crying, yelling and healing. My children were also keeping a close eye on me, planning outings and trying to be there for me, their love fully evident through their tender gestures.

I felt the pangs of loneliness, sadness, rejection and fear. Fear of the future, fear of the unknown. What was going to happen to me? The rejection had been in the making for years now, and it was just getting worse. There was rejection from my job, my upbringing, most of the men in my life and all of this caused me to lose confidence over the years. But the worst was carrying that shame and guilt again over using drugs to cope. Losing my dad, my complete support system, and Jesse was now coupled with the heaviness of dishonor, and it was easy to hide away in the therapist's office or at home.

I continued to work putting one foot in front of the other, and most days, that was all I could do. Four months later, in October of 2010, our new CEO asked me to transfer to the new hospital we opened, the one I was earlier going to manage, only this time I didn't have to be over both. He informed me the chief pulmonary doctor was specifically requesting me, a nice feather in my cap. I was a hard worker, a perfectionist of sorts, ran a very tight ship, and I had employees who had been loyal and followed me around, so even I could see why he would want me. However, I heard about all the problems they were having at this hospital, that the doctors were very upset over the mismanagement and poor care. It seemed like it would be a lot of stress and I wondered if I needed the stress with everything I had gone through that year. Reluctantly, I went.

From the beginning I could see it wasn't going to be easy. A lot of the staff was employees and friends of the former CEO, and I felt the tension from the start. During one meeting, the softball coordinator asked every female in the room, excluding me, to come out and play, and once again, I felt the pain of rejection. Not knowing what to do with it, I suffered again in silence.

My new boss didn't want to give me an office, but I stood my ground. He and I bumped heads from the start and I could see what a challenge laid ahead. He micromanaged everything I did. He would open the door to our department and look in several times a day, just to see if my staff was working. I believed that was my job. And he began making comments about my salary, saying it was too high and that no other manager made as much. After a few months he discontinued my bonus and reduced my annual raise.

As a result, my self esteem was taking a beating and I was getting sick every five to six weeks with shingles. My inability to ever leave the things or people that weren't working for me was taking its toll. The doctor gave me an anti-anxiety medication due to the enormous amount of stress I was under, and it set off the addiction allergy, again.

For awhile I managed to take the medication without consequences. Throughout the year though, from time to time, I would remember I was an addict, stop taking it, get sick again, take it and so forth. The insanity was in full swing. At the time I didn't have any support from my twelve step meetings to remind me I was an addict, and I sank further and further into the abyss. Miserable and suffering, I followed up with my therapy. I continued to attend church and began going to bible study on a regular basis. I was doing my best to cope however one thing was lacking. It was the only thing that could help a person like me, and I had given them up, twelve step meetings.

In June 2011, sick again with shingles, I arrived at work after taking the medication the night before, but with it still in my system, it showed in my eyes. My boss called me into his office and asked, "Is there something going on, you seem a little off today?"

"No I am fine," came my reply, wondering if I could trust him and be honest.

"Fran I know you, and there is something going on, your eyes look droopy and your gait is off."

As best I could I attempted to tell him the truth.

"I have told you on several occasions that I keep getting sick with shingles, and now the doctor has prescribed anti-anxiety medication, so I took it last night and I believe because I don't take this kind of medication ever, it affected or stayed with me longer."

"Okay," he said, and dismissed me, warning me to be careful at work.

Feeling relieved that I had been honest but at the same time trying to be true to me, I admitted to myself that I shouldn't be taking this medication, it didn't matter that I was taking it as prescribed, I was an addict and should never ever take this kind of medication.

Two weeks later, I showed up again the same way and under the same circumstance; I had taken the medication the night before, but still gave the appearance of improper behavior. I had a run in with a co-worker during a code blue setting, where I was consoling a family member who had just lost a loved one, when this woman came down the hall screaming, "What's wrong with you, are you taking pain pills?"

Horrified at her lack of professionalism, I went to my boss, reporting her inappropriateness, but it backfired. He took one look at me and asked the HR manager to get a drug screen and suspend me, pending the results.

On June 27, 2011, at home waiting on the call from work I realized I had enough. Thinking about the last year, the year since my dad died, I quickly saw what all was lost. I lost my father to begin with, not a perfect dad, but my dad. I lost Jesse, not a perfect man either, but my man. I lost my support system, my lifeline to wellness, all at the expense of giving up this unhealthy relationship. And I lost the last of my own confidence through circumstances all around me. My self-esteem was nonexistent, no where to be found.

I was sick. I was tired. I knew I was done. That morning, writing as I always did, I journaled these words, "Be the shepherd carrying me, break my legs if you have to" as I finally surrendered and asked God to step in. I called my sponsor and made a plan, and no sooner than I had, I received the call that I had been fired; the sweetest call of my life. Immediately, I knew God answered my morning prayer.

That evening, I ran to a new twelve step club, reached out and the hand of help was there. God placed everything I needed right at my disposal. I could feel the love that had eluded me my whole life, recognized that it had always been there, I just couldn't stop the chaos long enough to see or hear Him. I knew since my dad passed, that I had been broken open, laid out before the Almighty and was now asking Him to please do a mighty work in me.

Since that hot June day, I have been able to acknowledge that I didn't lose, I won. I won me back. And all that I thought I lost were actually gains, they were mere lessons in the journey we call life. I finally stopped and retreated, got away from the noise, and then I reviewed it all and have now begun redirecting my life to make it about serving Him. However by serving Him, I am serving others. By loving Him, I am loving others. And by writing this book, it is my love letter to Him.

He is Jehovah Rapha, the Lord our Healer, and as He opened the door for me, he will for you too. Through all the tragedy in my life, the one thing that was constant was God, although I didn't know it. He was loving me and watching over me, patiently waiting on me. I hope you find Him in the pages of this text and realize He has a plan for you. The God I serve sees us all equally, loves us all equally and desires His best for us. I am filled with gratitude for the road I have traveled, and admit that I have so much more to learn, that my journey is not over yet, and I look forward to it, walking with Him. I am finally free.

EPILOGUE

For if you forgive men when they sin against you, your heavenly Father will also forgive you

Matthew 6:14

I THOUGHT LONG AND HARD about what I wanted to say at the end of this project, what I wanted to leave you, the reader with. I prayed and asked God for help. The ending of this book was the hardest part to write because I, like all of us, am on a journey and although my journey isn't over, the end of the book is here and I had to close it out.

I reviewed the lessons that I've learned thus far in my life, and in order to wrap it up, I related to something Miss Oprah Winfrey inquired of each guest at the end of her show. She would ask them, "What is the one thing you know for sure" as she would wind down the interviews, and I thought, *That's it, that's what I'll do, I'll list the things I know for sure*, relieved to have worked it out.

In all my years on this earth, and through all the tragic things I have endured, all the happiness and sadness I've been able to experience, I know for sure, without any uncertainty, that God is REAL. Not only is He alive and well, He loves us, His creation, more than we can even wrap our minds around. The apostle Paul said to the church in Corinth, "Now we see but a poor reflection as in a mirror; then we shall see face to face. Now I know in part; then I shall know fully, even as I am fully known" (1Cor 13:12). I look forward to that day, with God in Heaven, to know fully, and to see the way that he sees. While here on earth though, God has given each one of us gifts, and my extraordinary faith is to help inspire, lift others up and help them see God.

As parents we want to raise children that we can be proud of, but more importantly, we need to raise children that are confident and sure of themselves. My story is a prime example of what happens to a child when they do not receive unconditional love, when no one hugs them or tells them they are pretty and can do great things. They need the basics, that's true, but just as vital, if not more so, is love. This I know to be true.

When someone is hurt or angered, they tend to want to lash out at the person or thing that hurt them. That kind of anguish can and does ruin lives. What I know for sure today is that no one ever intentionally set out to hurt me, they were all doing the best they could. The poet Maya Angelou said, "When you know better, you do better," and there is peace in accepting this truth.

Fear paralyzes; it desecrates. Fear is the weapon of the evil one. What I know for sure, beyond a shadow of a doubt, is that most people reside in some measure of fear. Some live in it, while others move in and out of it. It can disrupt and destroy us. Faith is the opposite of fear and when I sense fear, I quickly ask God for his strength. Remember, when all else fails, and the devil reminds you of your past, remind him of his future.

We all can get worried about how we will pay the bills, will we ever meet that special someone, do "they" like me or what our future holds. Today I am sure that my faith in God answers all these questions in the affirmative.

By tithing I have proven to myself, and I hope to you, that my financial worries are history. That being said, I know a lot of you can't wrap your head around this promise, it took me awhile too, so just do what it says in Malachi 3:10 and see that God is faithful.

I am also sure that nothing is as important to me as God's plan because I know what a mess I made when I was living in my own free will. In Matthew 6, Jesus said, do not worry about your life, what you will eat or drink, about your body or what you will wear, but seek first God's kingdom and righteousness and all these things will given to you as well. The more you are surrounded with like minded people, seeking becomes effortless.

Convinced now that it no longer matters if "they" like me, I like me. I no longer put my worth in what others think of me, fully aware of the damage and pain that lie caused in my life and happy to be free.

And I know for sure that the way to true happiness is by serving God and others. It has been said by many but until you experience it, you cannot completely understand this reality.

Most importantly, I accept that I hold the most awesome title, daughter of the King. My Father is a King, the most powerful of all, and I relish my position as His daughter. He has performed miracles on my behalf, loved me unconditionally, promises to care for me, and will allow me to spend eternity with Him; I no longer have to fear physical death.

I hope you can see that I've not cornered the market on

God, that anyone can have what I have. Go to him, he will meet you right where you are and I promise you won't be sorry. May God bless you and keep you.

91ˢᵗ PSALM

He who dwells in the shelter of the Most High
will rest in the shadow of the Almighty.
I will say of the Lord,"He is my refuge and my fortress,
my God, in whom I trust."

Surely he will save you from the fowler's snare
and from the deadly pestilence.
He will cover you with his feathers,
and under his wings you will find refuge;
his faithfulness will be your shield and rampart.
You will not fear the terror of night,
nor the arrow that flies by day,
nor the pestilence that stalks in the darkness,
nor the plague that destroys at midday.
A thousand may fall at your side,
ten thousand at your right hand,
but it will not come near you.
You will only observe with your eyes
and see the punishment of the wicked.

If you make the Most High your dwelling-
even the Lord, who is my refuge-
then no harm will befall you,
no disaster will come near your tent.
For he will command his angels concerning you

to guard you in all your ways;
they will lift you up in their hands,
so that you will not strike your foot against a stone.
You will tread upon the lion and the cobra;
you will trample the great lion and the serpent.

"Because he loves me," says the Lord, "I will rescue him;
I will protect him, for he acknowledges my name.
He will call upon me and I will answer him;
I will be with him in trouble,
I will deliver him and honor him.
With long life will I satisfy him
and show him my salvation."

REFERENCES

1. According to the *2009 AARC Respiratory Therapist Human Resource Study*, there are 12,373 licensed respiratory therapists in the state of Texas. This was based on information obtained from the Texas Licensure Board.
2. "Scripture taken from HOLY BIBLE, NEW INTERNATIONAL VERSION®. Copyright © 1973, 1978, 1984 by International Bible Society. Used by permission of Zondervan. All rights reserved."
3. www.1960sflashback.com
4. http://www.stmary.ws/highschool/physics/97/EGENOV.HTM
5. http://www.hear-the-world.com/en/the-magazine/title-story/archive/motown/part-1-50-years-of-motown
6. http://en.wikipedia.org/wiki/To_Kill_a_Mockingbird
7. http://www.timewarpmemories.com/top60shows
8. http://www.goodreads.com/author/quotes/3503.Maya Angelou